Palgrave Science Fiction and Fantasy: A New Canon

Series Editors
Sean Guynes, Michigan Publishing, University of
Michigan–Ann Arbor, Ann Arbor, USA
Keren Omry, Department of English, University of Haifa,
Haifa, Israel

W0235275

Palgrave Science Fiction and Fantasy: A New Canon provides short introductions to key works of science fiction and fantasy (SFF) speaking to why a text, trilogy, or series matters to SFF as a genre as well as to readers, scholars, and fans. These books aim to serve as a go-to resource for thinking on specific texts and series and for prompting further inquiry. Each book will be less than 30,000 words and structured similarly to facilitate classroom use. Focusing specifically on literature, the books will also address film and TV adaptations of the texts as relevant. Beginning with background and context on the text's place in the field, the author and how this text fits in their oeuvre, and the socio-historical reception of the text, the books will provide an understanding of how students, readers, and scholars can think dynamically about a given text. Each book will describe the major approaches to the text and how the critical engagements with the text have shaped SFF. Engaging with classic works as well as recent books that have been taken up by SFF fans and scholars, the goal of the series is not to be the arbiters of canonical importance, but to show how sustained critical analysis of these texts might bring about a new canon. In addition to their suitability for undergraduate courses, the books will appeal to fans of SFF.

Robert T. Tally Jr.

J. R. R. Tolkien's
The Hobbit

Realizing History Through Fantasy:
A Critical Companion

palgrave
macmillan

Robert T. Tally Jr.
Texas State University
San Marcos, TX, USA

ISSN 2662-8562   ISSN 2662-8570   (electronic)
Palgrave Science Fiction and Fantasy: A New Canon
ISBN 978-3-031-11265-2   ISBN 978-3-031-11266-9   (eBook)
https://doi.org/10.1007/978-3-031-11266-9

Cover illustration: Pictorial Press Ltd/Alamy Stock Photo. Courtesy of New Line Productions

This Palgrave Macmillan imprint is published by the registered company Springer Nature Switzerland
AG
The registered company address is: Gewerbestrasse 11, 6330 Cham, Switzerland

Unglücklich das Land, das keine Helden hat ...
Nein. Unglücklich das Land, das Helden nötig hat.

—Brecht

For my brothers,
Richey and Jay

Series Preface

The infinite worlds of science fiction and fantasy (SFF) dance along the borders between the possible and the impossible, the familiar and the strange, the immediate and the ever-approaching horizon. Speculative fiction in all its forms has been considered a genre, a medium, a mode, a practice, a compilation of themes or a web of assertions. With this in mind, *Palgrave Science Fiction and Fantasy: A New Canon* offers an expansive and dynamic approach to thinking SFF, destabilizing notions of the canon, so long associated with privilege, power, class, and hegemony. We take canon not as a singular and unchallenged authority but as shifting and thoughtful consensus among an always-growing collective of readers, scholars, and writers.

The cultural practice and production of speculation has encompassed novels, stories, plays, games, music, comics, and other media, with a lineage dating back at least to the nineteenth-century precursors through to the most recent publications. Existing scholarship has considered some of these media extensively, often with particular focus on film and TV. It is for this reason that *Palgrave Science Fiction and Fantasy* will forgo the cinematic and televisual, aspiring to direct critical attention at the other nodes of SFF expression.

Each volume in the series introduces, contextualizes, and analyzes a single work of SFF that ranges from the acknowledged "classic" to the should-be-classic, and asks two basic, but provocative questions: Why does this text matter to SFF? and *Why does (or should) this text matter to SFF readers, scholars, and fans?* Thus, the series joins into conversation both with scholars and students of the field to examine the parameters of SFF studies and the changing valences of fundamental categories like genre, medium, and canon. By emphasizing the critical approaches and major questions each text inspires, the series aims to offer "go-to" books for thinking about, writing on, and teaching major works of SFF.

Haifa, Israel   Keren Omry
Ann Arbor, USA   Sean Guynes

Preface and Acknowledgements

This book is intended as a critical introduction to J. R. R. Tolkien's *The Hobbit*, but it also advances an argument about the novel in the contexts of Tolkien's larger literary and philosophical project and of our own time. Although it may seem odd to put it this way, particularly given the canonical position it occupies within the fantasy genre, *The Hobbit* is ultimately a historical novel. It does not refer directly to any "real" historical events, of course, but it both enacts and conceptualizes history in a way that makes it real. Indeed, the *realization* of history, of our own place in history, is very much what the novel is all about. Tolkien's devotion to mythopoiesis is, in large part, impelled by a desire to bring the historical register to life via storytelling. The form of the heroic romance is thus both employed and subverted by Tolkien in his tale of a most unlikely hero, "quite a little fellow in a wide world," who nonetheless makes history.

The "realization" of history is an important aim of Tolkien's art. Tolkien's yearning for a mythic past, despite its clear nationalism and chauvinism at times, reflected a deep desire to connect his modern world with an august, barely accessible past through forms of historical narrative. This is not the "escape" into a mythical, premodern realm that is frequently imagined by fans and detractors of Tolkien's writing alike. Rather, despite the author's own embrace of the notion of *escape* in "On Fairy-Stories" and elsewhere, Tolkien's is an attempt to take the broken and disconnected fragments of culture and put them together into a meaningful history, evoking what he would call "the seamless web of story." Fredric Jameson, borrowing a phrase from Jean-François Lyotard, refers to this as "the desire called Marx," which is itself another way of saying the desire for narrative. Drawing upon Marxist and dialectical criticism, I read Tolkien's work, as it were, both with and against the grain, in order to disclose the ways that this historical project operates.

The Hobbit, first published in 1937, is a modern fantasy "classic," and yet within Tolkien's career it is an anomaly. Tolkien's primary areas of interest lay in the traditions of northern European mythology, history, and languages, and along with his scholarly and personal pursuits he was passionately devoted to the elaborate, lifelong project that unfolded across the diverse and protean materials that would make up *The Silmarillion* and other writings that were only posthumously published. Tolkien notoriously complained that "the hobbit" had *intruded* into that world. As he put it in one 1938 letter, "my mind on the 'story' side is really preoccupied with the 'pure' fairy stories or mythology of the *Silmarillion*, into which even Mr. Baggins got dragged against my original will" (*Letters* 38). Although he would claim that he had nothing more to say about hobbits, Tolkien grudgingly agreed to write a sequel, which became *The Lord of the Rings* (1954–1955), one of the bestselling and most influential works of fantasy ever. Thus, *The Hobbit* retrospectively became a "prequel"—something that repeated itself with somewhat grotesque results in the cinematic universe of the Peter Jackson-directed *Lord of the Rings* and *Hobbit* movie trilogies in the twenty-first century—after its original status as a standalone adventure story written for children. *The Hobbit* finds itself in a paradoxical situation in Tolkien's *oeuvre*: it is at once an absolutely central text *and* an outlier with respect to the larger *legendarium*.

The Hobbit contributes to and distinguishes itself from the materials that would make up *The Silmarillion*, as well as those of *The Lord of the Rings*, and becomes part of the overall History of Middle-earth, an archive enlarged by Christopher Tolkien through the posthumous publication of writings by his father that have appeared over the years. With respect to the latter, it is worthwhile situating *The Hobbit* historically in the interwar period of British history, amid the looming geopolitical crises, and in relation to the views of a relatively young Oxford professor of Anglo-Saxon philology, who wrote delightful tales for his children (such as *The Father Christmas Letters*) and indulged in other creative writing, especially contributions to what he called his "private and beloved nonsense," in his spare time. The emergence of *The Hobbit* and of Bilbo Baggins from his comfortable hobbit hole at this particular moment was, in fact, rather momentous.

In this book, I focus mostly on *The Hobbit* alone, apart from *The Lord of the Rings* and other works, in keeping with the plan of the *Palgrave Science Fiction and Fantasy: A New Canon* series. Moreover, I do not assume that all readers will be familiar with Tolkien's other writings, especially the increasingly vast treasury of posthumously published material, but I hope that Tolkien scholars and enthusiasts who are conversant in the larger body of the author's work will find my study of value as well.

In examining *The Hobbit*, I have divided my discussion into a few significant parts, for example, focusing on narrative style, genre and the ideology of form, the elaboration of the otherworldly spaces of Middle-earth, and the characterizations of its peoples, with particular reference to the question of race. This is inherently selective, as one can imagine, and the choice to focus on these aspects of the novel is motivated in part by a desire to show how Tolkien's historical project coheres with respect to form and content, which are so closely integrated as to be effectively inseparable. My treatment is far from exhaustive, and there are whole libraries' worth of scholarly and critical studies devoted to *The Hobbit*. Because this brief study is intended as an introduction, I have refrained from including too much scholarly apparatus, including footnotes or extensive citation of secondary sources. I hope that the selections in the bibliography can help to make up for this loss, a least a bit, but I know that a great deal of important research on Tolkien remains unmentioned here. I would therefore encourage readers interested in this work to explore the rich treasury of Tolkien Studies on their own.

I have had the good fortune to be able to teach *The Hobbit* and other works by Tolkien in courses at Texas State University, and I would like to thank my students and colleagues for their contributions to my thinking about these matters over the years. My indebtedness to the generous community of scholars cannot be measured, and I am grateful to the many friends, colleagues, and critics who have helped me along the way, including (but not limited to) Gerry Canavan, Jane Chance, Cait Coker, Janet Brennan Croft, Merve Emre, Dimitra Fimi, Verlyn Flieger, Fredric Jameson, Youngmin Kim, John D. Rateliff, Robin Anne Reid, and Phillip E. Wegner. I thank Reiko Graham for putting up with me during most of the time I have been writing and for much longer too. While working on this book we lost the company of Dusty Britches, sadly, but I am happy to have the support of Windy Britches, Steve French, and Nigel Tuffnail. The book is dedicated to my younger brothers, Richey and Jay, with whom I have enjoyed seemingly endless conversations about Middle-earth and the goings-on there. I look forward to talking with them some more.

A Note on the Texts

For ease of reference and in deference to the massive popularity of Tolkien's work, I have chosen to use the trade paperback editions of his novels wherever possible. The definitive edition of *The Hobbit* can be found in *The Annotated Hobbit*, edited by Douglas A. Anderson, and supplemented by John D. Rateliff's *The History of the Hobbit*, a magnificent achievement incorporating different drafts, notes, and other materials, along with superlative commentary and criticism. I heartily recommend that work to all, but I am aware that most people read Tolkien in the form of inexpensive paperbacks. I also trust that professional Tolkien scholars, along with many devoted fans, will have no trouble finding my references regardless of the edition. Unless otherwise noted, my references to *The Hobbit* are to the revised, finalized version, featuring the Gollum most of us know so well. Also, following a convention in Tolkien Studies, I use the term "Silmarillion" (in quotation marks) with reference to the wide-ranging, heterogenous materials of Tolkien's larger *legendarium*, in order to distinguish it from *The Silmarillion*, curated, "regularized," and made coherent by Christopher Tolkien, but published as a singular work by J. R. R. Tolkien alone in 1977.

San Marcos, USA   Robert T. Tally Jr.

Praise for *J. R. R. Tolkien's* The Hobbit

"This guide combines an introduction to *The Hobbit's* significance to both Tolkien's legendarium and fantasy in general with fresh theoretical approaches to the text. Tally uses the tools of historicism, narrative theory, Marxism, and geocriticism (among others) to help the reader better understand this not-so-simple classic of children's fantasy. His application of these varied theoretical approaches to the enduring question of race in Tolkien's work is particularly valuable in our current climate."

—Janet Brennan Croft, *Associate University Librarian, University of Northern Iowa, USA, and editor of the journal* Mythlore

"Robert T. Tally Jr.'s book deals with a very well-known novel–J. R. R. Tolkien's *The Hobbit* – that is simultaneously a foundational text within Tolkien's work and an anomalous outlier, just as hobbits themselves have always felt slightly out of place in the wider world of Middle-earth despite playing a central role in its fate. Tally addresses this ambiguous status from several angles, in a work that is both highly readable and securely founded in Tolkien scholarship."

—Dr. Catherine Butler, *Reader in English Literature, Cardiff University, UK*

"Tally's study of *The Hobbit* is a whirlwind tour of Middle-earth from below, charted by Marx, Benjamin, Jameson, and Brecht, uncovering what the history, ideology, and politics of that strange place might teach us about our own much stranger one."

—Gerry Canavan, *Marquette University, President of the Science Fiction Research Association*

"Tally shows how Tolkien's first published novel was both anomalous with the rest of his vast legendarium, yet remains foundational within it. An outlying text, then, may benefit from an outlying critical lens, and here Tally deploys his expertise in Marxist and dialectical criticism to read The Hobbit in valuable new ways — both with and against the grain, as he says — offering insights into style, narrative form, race, class, historicity, and more."

—Jason Fisher, *Author of* Tolkien and the Study of His Sources: Critical Essays (2011)

Contents

1

Introduction: *In a Hole in the Ground …*

Has there ever been a less welcome guest, and one who later becomes so very beloved? I do not mean Gandalf, who irritates Bilbo Baggins in the opening pages of *The Hobbit* by imposing an unwanted adventure upon him. Nor do I mean Thorin Oakenshield or the twelve other dwarves who make up the "unexpected party" in the novel's first chapter. I mean *the* hobbit himself, Bilbo, and by extension, moreover, the book that he stars in.

Bilbo's arrival onto the scene of J. R. R. Tolkien's imagination was almost purely accidental, as has been related in the legendary anecdote about a poor professor's dull labors over a pile of student exams. As Tolkien related the oft-told "origin story" in a 1955 letter to W. H. Auden,

> All I remember about the start of *The Hobbit* is sitting correcting School Certificate papers in the everlasting weariness of that annual task forced on impecunious academics with children. On a blank leaf I scrawled: "In

© The Author(s), under exclusive license to Springer Nature
Switzerland AG 2022
R. T. Tally Jr., *J. R. R. Tolkien's* The Hobbit,
Palgrave Science Fiction and Fantasy: A New Canon,
https://doi.org/10.1007/978-3-031-11266-9_1

a hole in the ground there lived a hobbit." I did not and do not know why. I did nothing about it, for a long time, and for some years I got no further than the production of Thrór's Map. But it became *The Hobbit* in the early 1930s, and was eventually published. (*Letters* 215)

The full story may be a bit more complicated, since Tolkien had already for some years been coming up with tales for his own children's amusement, not to mention the fact that he had been almost constantly working on and over the "Elvish Legends" and the "History of the Gnomes" that make up his "Silmarillion," a lifelong and never entirely finished project. But it is clear that *the* hobbit, Bilbo Baggins, was an intruder, and that the emergence of a bestselling, now thoroughly canonical work of children's literature—indeed, world literature, beloved by readers of all ages—was quite accidental.

Bilbo's incursion into the elaborate history of Middle-earth is thus all the more extraordinary for its having been somewhat adventitious or at least unplanned for. The story was written as a children's book, something Tolkien later regretted, lamenting his decision to employ a "silliness of manner" he had then—and in his view, erroneously—deemed suitable for children's stories (*Letters* 215). *The Hobbit* was the first work of fiction published by Tolkien. At the time, he was a 45-year-old professor of Anglo-Saxon philology at Oxford University. But he had been working on his grander *legendarium* since his own youth, not to mention his academic writings, translations, and tales invented for his own children such as *The Father Christmas Letters* (published posthumously). Thus for Tolkien, as well as for the readers of the world, *The Hobbit* also came as an unexpected visitor, if not an unwelcome one.

Tolkien later expressed some regret about bringing Bilbo Baggins into the middle of his "private and beloved nonsense," the sprawlingly vast *legendarium* containing the myths, songs, tales, languages, and histories of his imaginary Otherworld, which is also in some respects "our" own world. But this unforeseen addition to that universe actually brought Tolkien's Middle-earth into public view, revealing its distinctive landscapes and characters, and serving as the point of departure for what would become arguably the most influential single novel of the twentieth century, *The Lord of the Rings*. Beloved, did I say? That seems relatively modest praise for this hobbit, who went from an unexpected intruder into the musings of a storytelling philologist to a legendary hero and a foundational character for an entire literary genre. It is as if Bilbo Baggins really did emerge out of nowhere, as if from a hole in the ground, but from this inauspicious beginning, there can be no doubt that he made history.

There and Back Again

The story of *The Hobbit* is quite well known, but a brief plot summary may be useful. The narrative itself is rather episodic, with almost every chapter containing its own mini-adventure, but the cumulative effect is significant. This is most visible in the overall competence and confidence of *the* hobbit, Bilbo, who is comically unsuited for the places in which he finds himself during the first parts of the novel, but by the end is arguably the leader of his company and a more generally *worldly* individual. Roughly two-thirds of the narrative cover Bilbo's journey to the Lonely Mountain, while the last third deals with the dragon, the aftermath of his slaying, the Battle of Five Armies, and the return home.

As the story begins, Bilbo Baggins is a simple, ordinary, and self-satisfied hobbit, who despite being a "hobbit"—with that people's distinctive characteristics, such as dwelling in comfortable, well-appointed holes in the ground or going about unshod on their tough-soled, hair-covered feet—lives the life of an Edwardian, bourgeois Englishman in a relatively bucolic region approximating the West Midlands of Tolkien's own youth. A *hobbit*, we learn, is for the most part a diminutive branch of the *human* race, roughly half the size. Allegorically, as Tolkien asserted, hobbits are made small "partly to exhibit the pettiness of man, plain unimaginative parochial man […] and mostly to show up, in creatures of small physical power, the amazing and unexpected heroism of ordinary men 'in a pinch'" (*Letters* 158). Bilbo's peaceful, uneventful life gets its first real challenge when Gandalf, the wandering wizard, visits and enlists him in "an adventure."

The humorous opening chapter of *The Hobbit* features "an unexpected party," as thirteen dwarves along with Gandalf show up for dinner.

Bilbo discovers that he is to join them as a burglar, otherwise known as an "expert treasure-hunter" (19), thus breaking up the group's unlucky number thirteen and otherwise contributing to the success of their quest. Here the reader also learns that Bilbo himself is of two minds, figured forth as hereditary characteristics from his father's and mother's lines respectively: the stolid, sensible, and unadventurous Baggins side is countered by the wilder Tookish character of his mother, Belladonna Took, and her family. Whenever Bilbo feels adventurous or takes chances, his "Tookish" side is coming out, although by the end of the novel, arguably, he has reconciled his two halves, almost like Goethe's Wilhelm Meister, whose heralded "apprenticeship" ends where his artistic and bourgeois temperaments find lasting harmony. Despite his misgiving and surprising even himself, Bilbo joins Thorin and Company on their mission to return to Thorin's ancestral home at the Lonely Mountain far to the east, to reclaim that kingdom from the dragon Smaug.

The following ten chapters involve one key incident after another, and each chapter seems to introduce a new character or race of characters. Thus, Bilbo encounters hideous trolls, anthropomorphic creatures with rustic English accents and ordinary names (William, Bert, and Tom), from whom he and the dwarves barely escape, thanks to Gandalf's clever intervention. Then they meet the elves of Rivendell, whose leader is Elrond, wisest of lore-masters in Middle-earth. Afterward they see stone giants in the Misty Mountains, where they are captured by goblins (known in Tolkien's other writings as "orcs"). Bilbo becomes separated from the others at this point, discovers what turns out to be a magic ring, and meets Gollum, a unique creature, with whom he plays a "riddle game." The finding of that ring "was a turning point in his career" (68), and in Tolkien's as well, for the magic ring that grants Bilbo invisibly, thus aiding him greatly in his adventures to come, would become the crucial device at the center of Tolkien's magnum opus, *The Lord of the Rings*, the vast sequel to *The Hobbit*. Escaping from Gollum's subterranean lair, Bilbo rejoins Gandalf and the dwarves—Gandalf had killed the Great Goblin and led the dwarves to safety—outside on the eastern part of the mountains. But there they are menaced by goblins and wargs ("or so the evil wolves over the Edge of the Wild are called" [101]), before being rescued by eagles, who take them to their eyrie. The eagles then deposit the company at the Carrock, in the land of Beorn, a "skin-changer" who can take the form of a great bear or a large man (116), and Beorn aids them in their journey to the edge of Mirkwood. At this point, Gandalf leaves the company to deal with business elsewhere. In the forest, they are attacked by giant spiders, and Bilbo is able to save the others, but before they can escape, they are captured by wood-elves, "more dangerous and less wise" than the elves of Rivendell (167), who imprison the dwarves. Bilbo, employing his ring to stay invisible, eludes capture, and eventually crafts a plan to rescue the dwarves by loading them into empty wine barrels, which float down the river to Lake-town, where they receive a "warm welcome" from the people, who believe that the prosperity prophesied to accompany the return of the "King under the Mountain" was at hand (197). At last, in Chapter XI, Bilbo and the dwarves arrive at the Lonely Mountain.

Thereafter, the story is no longer about a journey, but about dealing with the dragon, and then dealing with the aftermath of the dragon's demise. They discover the hidden entrance to the mountain, which itself had involved a long process by which Gandalf had come to possess Thrór's Map (i.e., the map belonging to Thorin's grandfather) and accompanying key, Elrond had translated the secret message written in "moon-letters" on the map, and Bilbo had noticed the thrush "knocking" on the stones just in time for the keyhole to be revealed. Bilbo then sneaks into the treasure room, where the dragon lay sleeping, and takes a single cup; returning, he finds that Smaug was not asleep, and while wearing the ring Bilbo engages him in conversation, during which Bilbo notices one weak, unarmored spot on the dragon's breast. That is significant, since the thrush overhears Bilbo's mention of this bare patch, and delivers that news to Bard the bowman, who in Lake-town eventually slays the dragon by shooting an arrow into that spot, but not before the dragon has destroyed the town. In some stories, the killing of the dragon might be the climax, if not the end of the tale, but Tolkien clearly recognizes that this event has rather perilous consequences, for a mountain of gold is now presumably unguarded. This sets the stage for the Battle of Five Armies, in which Thorin and company are joined by an army of dwarves from the Iron Hills; the men of Dale (with Bard, the dragon-slayer, as their king) and the elves of Mirkwood join forces to demand their share of the treasure. Taking the dwarves' most treasured jewel, the Arkenstone (which is perhaps a nod to Tolkien's *Silmarils*), as a bargaining chip, Bilbo attempts to broker a deal that would prevent open war, but then an army of goblins and wolves from the North, incensed by the killing of the Great Goblin, attacks. The dwarves, elves, and men unite to fight the common enemy, and they are eventually aided by the eagles and Beorn, who turn the tide of battle in their favor. Bilbo, who had been knocked unconscious by a falling stone, missed much of the battle, but upon awaking, he discovers that the victory has come with a cost. Fili and Kili were slain, and Thorin lies dying, a bitter ending for Bilbo who was at least able to make peace with the dwarf king in the end. In the final chapter, Bilbo and Gandalf make the return journey, for, as Bilbo puts it, "out back is to legends and we are coming home" (301).

In the novel's final scene, which takes place "some years afterwards," Bilbo Baggins is writing his memoirs: "he thought of calling them 'There and Back Again, a Hobbit's Holiday'" (304). Notably, the full title of Tolkien's book is called *The Hobbit, or, There and Back Again*, which allows for the quirky blurring of authorship, between Tolkien and Bilbo. (Obviously, the narrative voice makes the idea that Bilbo is simply telling his own story seem ludicrous, but then Bilbo is an odd fellow.) Ever the stickler, Tolkien later developed a backstory that allowed *The Hobbit* and *The Lord of the Rings* to maintain a sense of historic and hobbitic authenticity, while also explaining why we in the twentieth century were receiving this text from an Oxford professor named Tolkien. That is, as I discuss in the next chapter, he conceived of these tales as having been written by Bilbo (and later Frodo and Sam) in "The Red Book of Westmarch," which Tolkien merely translated. That conceit alone indicates the degree to which Tolkien wished for his fantasy fiction to register with the reader as intensely historical. But Bilbo's title, which self-effacingly characterizes what at times was a terribly dangerous, exciting, and world-transformative adventure as a mere "holiday," a brief vacation away from normal routine, is typical of the humility and down-to-earthiness of hobbits, which is itself part of Tolkien's vision of history in which "the great policies of world history, 'the wheels of the world,' are often turned not by Lords and Governors, even gods, but by the seemingly unknown and weak" (*Letters* 149). Bilbo Baggins's adventures include "world-historical" events and individuals, in Hegel's sense, but they are also undertaken by an ordinary person, "quite a little fellow in a wide world," as Gandalf calls him (305). "There and Back Again" is thus a suitably quotidian title for such a grand adventure tale, in which an utterly unremarkable person, ill-fit for heroics and unsuited for epic romance, makes history.

A Hobbit in All but Size

Bilbo's creator made history as well. Tolkien's biography is well known to most fans and scholars. He was even the subject of a 2019 bio-pic, directed by Dome Karukoski and simply titled *Tolkien*, which focuses on the early part of his life's story, culminating in a scene in which he writes that famous first line of *The Hobbit* on a blank sheet of an examination paper. Given that choice, one might imagine that the film's writers had imagined Tolkien's personal story as being something of a prologue to his career as a writer, for when *the* hobbit enters the scene, the movie ends. It is perhaps just as well that the film ends there, since the life of a university professor and writer who is actively writing may not prove very interesting, filled as the days are with sitting at a desk and scribbling. It is also apt that Tolkien's story seems to end at the very moment that the hobbit's story begins, for as Tolkien himself confessed, "I am in fact a *Hobbit* (in all but size)" (*Letters* 288), and so the drama of his own story can be easily displaced onto the far more entertaining adventures of the hobbits after the mid-1930s.

Tolkien was born in 1892 to English parents in Bloemfontein, South Africa, where his father worked as a manager of a British bank. Tolkien's father died while a three-year-old Tolkien and his mother were visiting family in England, so rather than returning to Africa, they settled in the West Midlands. At age 12, Tolkien lost his mother, and under the guardianship of Father Francis Xavier Morgan, he attended King Edward's School in Birmingham. In 1911, he enrolled in Exeter College, Oxford University, graduating in 1915. Meanwhile, he had met Edith Bratt, to whom he became engaged in 1913, and they were married in

1916; they would have four children together: John, Michael, Christopher, and Priscilla. During the First World War, Tolkien served in the Lancaster Fusiliers, eventually taking part in the Battle of Somme in France. There he developed a case of "trench fever," and he was returned to England to recover, thus sparing him the worst of the fighting. Nearly everyone in his battalion was killed, and most of Tolkien's university friends perished in the war. Unsurprisingly, his experience with war greatly affected his views and influenced his depictions of soldiers in his later work (see, e.g., Garth, *Tolkien and the Great War*, 94–95).

After the war, Tolkien got a job working for the *Oxford English Dictionary*, focusing especially on Germanic words beginning with the letter "W." In 1920, he became a Reader at the University of Leeds, where he published a textbook, *A Middle English Vocabulary*, as well as a new translation of *Sir Gawain and the Green Knight*; during this time he also completed a translation of *Beowulf*, which was not published until 2014. In 1925, Tolkien returned to Oxford, where he became a Professor of Anglo-Saxon at Pembroke College. In 1945, he moved (within Oxford) to Merton College, serving as the Merton Professor of English Language and Literature until his retirement in 1959. Although he remains best known for his works of fantasy, his scholarship and even his teaching undoubtedly contributed to his creative writing. During his final decade, Tolkien continued to work on his lifelong project, the *legendarium* associated with the "Silmarillion," which he had begun writing in different forms as early as his teenage years. In the 1960s he considered writing a possible sequel to *The Lord of the Rings*, while he also tried to integrate and harmonize his published work with the heterogenous "Silmarillion" materials, much of which has been published in *The History of Middle-earth* (1983–1996), a twelve-volume collection of writings curated, edited, and annotated by his son Christopher Tolkien, who has also seen to the publication of numerous other posthumous works. J. R. R. Tolkien died in 1973.

In death, Tolkien's legend has only grown, as has his considerable body of work. In 1977, *The Silmarillion* was published as a single work *by* Tolkien, "edited by Christopher Tolkien," and it became the year's most popular work of fiction, topping the *New York Times* bestseller list for a remarkable 23 consecutive weeks from October 1977 to March 1978.

As Christopher Tolkien later lamented, *The Silmarillion* gave an artificial and misleading sense of continuity and even completion; in reality, it had been compiled by Christopher from materials written by his father across many decades, with numerous inconsistencies and revisions, as one might expect of such a vast assemblage of notes and drafts. Some of the difficulties associated with *The Silmarillion* can be attributed to this illusory coherence, as many of the texts included may not have been originally written for inclusion, in those forms, or with the exact ordering of things in the way that they are presented in the published volume. Indeed, it is clear that part of Christopher's aim in compiling *The Silmarillion* in the form that it took was to provide a supplement to *The Lord of the Rings*, but much of the "Silmarillion" materials had been written down even before *The Hobbit* and *The Lord of the Rings* were conceived.

After the publication of *The Silmarillion*, starting with the *Unfinished Tales of Númenor and Middle-earth* in 1980, and then extending to the monumental *History of Middle-earth* series, published between 1983 and 1996, Christopher attempted to rectify matters by revealing J. R. R. Tolkien's original drafts in all their sketchiness, along with Christopher's own commentary which tended to situate those drafts in relation to his father's biography and to his other writings. More recently, Christopher and the Tolkien Estate have come out with additional books, including three extended versions of major tales from *The Silmarillion* (or the "Silmarillion"): that is, the story of Húrin and his children, the adventures of Beren and Lúthian, and the narrative of the events leading to the fall of Gondolin. To these have been added a steady stream of other previously unpublished writings by Tolkien, including his translation of *Beowulf* and his juvenile retelling of the story of Kullervo, a character from the Finnish epic, the *Kalevala*, which is also a source for Tolkien's story of Túrin Turambar in *The Silmarillion*. Christopher himself died in 2020 at the age of 95, but even this has not stopped the flow of posthumous works, for *The Nature of Middle-earth*, edited by Carl F. Hostetter and featuring what the subtitle calls "late writings on the lands, inhabitants, and metaphysics of Middle-earth," appeared in 2021.

The Tolkien industry is inestimably enlarged and empowered by the growing presence of his work in mass media, particularly the celebrated film adaptations of *The Lord of the Rings* and *The Hobbit*, directed by

Peter Jackson, along with a new Amazon series (*The Rings of Power*), numerous video games, and so forth. Meanwhile, the popularity of the books themselves, particularly *The Hobbit* and *The Lord of the Rings*, remains as strong as ever. The unlikely story of a hobbit intruding upon an unassuming professor's "private and beloved nonsense" has had truly amazing consequences that have shaped twenty-first century culture globally.

The Fish Out of Water

The Hobbit is also an oddity in the history of world literature. A best-selling novel first published in 1937, *The Hobbit* maintains its place as a "classic" of both fantasy and children's literature. No matter how the terms are defined, Tolkien's novel is undeniably "canonical" with respect to those genres, and its place in modern British and world literature is equally secure. In a poll conducted by the BBC in 2003 as part of "The Big Read," aimed at discovering the "Nation's Best-Loved Novel," *The Hobbit* ranked 25th overall; famously (or infamously, in the view of some critics), its sequel, *The Lord of the Rings* was ranked number one. Even that bit of trivia is telling: for all its renown as an individual work, *The Hobbit* is perhaps best known today as the "prequel"—a word Tolkien would not have used—to its far more substantial and influential follow-up novel, *The Lord of the Rings*. That immense "modern epic," published in three volumes in 1954 and 1955, was initially prepared as a sequel to and thus a continuation of *The Hobbit*, but it quickly became a tale that "grew in the telling" (Tolkien, *Fellowship* viii), and retroactively overwhelmed its predecessor.

Indeed, in order to make *The Lord of the Rings* work *as* a sequel, Tolkien and his publisher altered the original text of *The Hobbit* in order "to bring the old story of Bilbo's adventure more strongly into accord with the new one of Frodo's quest" (Rateliff, *History* 731). Among other, more minor changes that appeared in the novel's fifth printing (or second edition) in 1951, Tolkien completely revised the memorable scene in which Bilbo finds the ring in Gollum's cavern. Originally, Gollum seemed perfectly willing to give Bilbo the ring as a prize for winning the riddle game, but failing that—since Bilbo had the ring in his pocket, after all—Gollum helpfully shows Bilbo the way out of the caverns. Once this magic ring that confers invisibility on the wearer becomes the One Ring of *The Lord of the Rings*, the chapter (along with Gollum's character) needed to be revised. The earlier version is then recast as the tale told initially by Bilbo regarding the finding of the ring, and the fact that an otherwise honest hobbit seems to have lied about its origin is itself taken as sign of the ring's malignancy.

Tolkien was tempted to change far more than that, for he became increasingly uneasy about the many ways that the original work did not fit in with the world he was trying to represent in his larger literary project. In fact, he did change things, but the extent of these alterations has only come to light in posthumous publications. Among the more notable efforts in this regard: Tolkien wrote an extensive, complementary narrative in 1954, "The Quest for Erebor," later published in *Unfinished Tales of Middle-earth and Númenor* (1980); he undertook some major revisions of the novel's text itself in 1960, and that new material was unveiled only in 1987 by Christopher Tolkien at a conference and first published in print only in 2007 in John D. Rateliff's *The History of the Hobbit* (see 763–838); and, when asked by his publisher to make slight revisions in the mid-1960s—in a bizarre literary historical footnote, an "authoritative text" was needed in order to reassert U.S. copyright, for a "bootleg" version was published in 1965—Tolkien apparently found "a good deal" of *The Hobbit* to be so "very poor" that, according to his biographer, he "had to restrain himself from rewriting the entire book" (Carpenter, *Biography* 230). Hence, *The Hobbit* is an anomaly within Tolkien's *oeuvre*, at once a treasured masterpiece and a mildly embarrassing outlier, a classic standalone work of fantasy fiction that is somehow also an almost paratextual adjunct to an even more significant, "classic" novel.

The Hobbit undoubtedly could, and does, stand on its own as a marvelous adventure story aimed at a youthful audience, but with the publication of *The Lord of the Rings*, it was figuratively and literally transformed. *The Hobbit* is simultaneously essential to a much larger story and a rather ill-fitting contribution to it, since in its original composition, it was never intended as a "prologue" or even a contribution to the other materials. As Tolkien put it in a 1938 letter, the hobbit "intruded" into the grander history he had in mind, and Tolkien spent much of the rest of his life trying to reconcile such an unexpected occurrence with what he took to be his more valuable literary project, which from his own boyhood to his dying day remained the materials associated with the "Silmarillion." Indeed, when invited to write a sequel to *The Hobbit*, Tolkien initially sent his publisher what he had of the "Silmarillion," which was rejected, and even as *The Lord of the Rings* was about to appear, Tolkien desperately wished to publish his "Silmarillion" alongside it, viewing the ensemble as a single, vast narrative, the Saga of the Jewels and the Rings.

The apparently adventitious arrival of Bilbo Baggins onto the scene of Tolkien's career is, in what might be called a dialectical reversal or ruse of history in its own right, a profoundly significant event, for without *The Hobbit* there would have been no call for its sequel, and without the success of both *The Hobbit* and *The Lord of the Rings*, there likely would have been little desire on the parts of publishers and readers to explore in greater detail the rich history and geography of Middle-earth to be found in the posthumously published works. In 1938, Tolkien understandably wished to be done with Bilbo, whose final destiny—"he remained happy to the end of his days, and those were extraordinarily long" (304)—appeared to have been written already, after all. Tolkien wanted to get back to the materials he was more interested in working on. As he wrote to his publisher, who had inquired about a sequel to *The Hobbit*, "I cannot think of anything more to say about *hobbits*. Mr. Baggins seems to have exhibited so fully both the Took and the Baggins side of their nature. But I have only too much to say, and much already written, about the world into which the hobbit intruded" (*Letters* 24). As it happens, however, this pertinacious little hobbit's intrusion is what brought that world into view for millions of readers. There are no hobbits whatsoever in the "Silmarillion," of course, but the story of a single hobbit was the impetus that brought this far grander history to light.

Ironically, perhaps, *The Hobbit*'s generic unsuitability for the discursive world of the "Silmarillion," and correspondingly Bilbo Baggins's lack of fit in the world he finds himself in throughout his adventures, are likely what make Tolkien's broader philosophical and political project of *realizing history* possible. As Tolkien put it in a 1943 letter to his son

Christopher, who was at the time chafing under the unpleasant demands of military survive during a world war, "I imagine the fish out of water is the only fish to have an inkling of water" (*Letters* 64). Bilbo Baggins certainly fits the bill as the metaphorical "fish out of water" throughout most of *The Hobbit*, but his pain and discomfort at finding himself in those situations brings him to realize the situation he is in, the part in a grander narrative he plays, wittingly or otherwise, and the degree to which he remains within the "world" itself. This is a variant on Fredric Jameson's famous observation from *The Political Unconscious* that "History is what hurts" (102), but there is also the sense that, in actively making history while being subject to historical forces far beyond one's ken, the "water" that is history is at least perceived, becoming knowable and meaningful.

That such historical consciousness would emerge from the relative comforts of a "hole in the ground" is not as surprising as some might think. This earthiness is crucial to the political unconscious of Tolkien's vision, in which the ideological structures of power and wealth dialectically interact with the utopian potential of radical democracy and what Adorno called a *Leben ohne Angst* ("a life without anxiety"). Bilbo's initial comfort and self-satisfaction at the beginning of *The Hobbit* reflects the sort of false consciousness that ensures that "history" remain occluded, or at the very least, remain the stuff of the mere past, unconnected to one's present day experiences. Whereas the "little fellow" who shares a smoke with Gandalf and Balin in the final scene of the novel, still amid his creature comforts in his tidy hole in the ground, is now fully conscious of the "wide world" of which, and of whose very constitution, he is himself a part. Bilbo has "made history," to be sure, but more importantly he has made history appear as *real*, bridging the chasm that had previously separated daily life and thought from distant legends. In this way, by "putting earth under the feet of 'romance'" as Tolkien put it (*Letters* 215), *The Hobbit* allows us to realize history anew, as well as our own place in history.

2

The Way to Talk to Dragons: Interpellation, Style, and Narrative Form

After many exciting, dangerous, and interesting adventures along the way from his cozy hobbit hole all the way to the Lonely Mountain, Bilbo Baggins at last confronts Smaug, the dragon that in many fantasy tales might have proved to be the final obstacle, the "Boss," in the argot of video gamers. (In its final chapters, *The Hobbit* impressively focuses attention of the troubling consequences of the elimination of the "Boss.") Speaking to the dragon, Bilbo tries carefully to engage in conversation without giving away too much information, which leads to an amusing dialogue, albeit one that takes place within a scene of deadly peril for the hobbit. In the midst of this conversation, the narrator comments: "This is the way to talk to dragons, if you don't want to reveal your proper name (which is wise), and don't want to infuriate them by a flat refusal (which is also very wise)" (*Hobbit* 223). This sort of intrusive, though instructive, interpellation by the narrator is something the reader would be quite familiar with by this point, and it speaks to Tolkien's style in this novel as well as to the overall effects of it in the narrative as a whole.

© The Author(s), under exclusive license to Springer Nature
Switzerland AG 2022
R. T. Tally Jr., *J. R. R. Tolkien's* The Hobbit,
Palgrave Science Fiction and Fantasy: A New Canon,
https://doi.org/10.1007/978-3-031-11266-9_2

The narrative voice in *The Hobbit* is quite striking. It is at once authoritative, belonging to one who so thoroughly knows this other-worldly world as to be able to speak with confidence but also in a rather matter-of-fact way about dealings with dragons, but it is also familiar and friendly, implicitly admitting the audience into the same sphere of authoritative knowledge. The reader, here named with the second-person pronoun—a "you" that could, as it seems to do at times in the narrative, stand for a particular person or persons, or that could serve as a more impersonal, general form (e.g., "one should not rouse the ire of dragons")—is presumably ignorant of the world of dragons, but is also positioned as one who, like Bilbo, is "not quite so unlearned in dragon-lore as all that" (222). The storyteller is not only someone who knows this particular story, but is a master of lore, steeped in broad and deep knowledge of the world in which the story unfolds. The reader, understandably, for the most part lacks such knowledge; the reader therefore receives the details of the story but, on occasion, is addressed directly by the narrator in a manner intended to clarify those details or help to make clearer sense of Middle-earth. In this manner, Tolkien's narrative voice in the novel helps to orient the reader toward a greater world-historical consciousness.

The style of *The Hobbit*, typified in part by its distinctive narrative voice and in part by the way it presents the voices of others in the text, is crucial in making its story so enchanting. But Tolkien himself regretted aspects of this mode of storytelling later on, as he recognized the far too familiar, avuncular, and anachronistic narrative voice to be out of alignment with the "high" style of many of his other writings. As with other jarring features, such as Thorin's absurdly anachronistic worry that "we shall be picked up by some giant and kicked sky-high for a football" (57), the narrative voice and its frequent use of direct address to the reader seem altogether out of place in the discourse of the heroic romance, featured in *The Lord of the Rings* and in the "Silmarillion." And yet, this apparently eccentric style of *The Hobbit* serves its purpose well, as it helps to bring this grand, historical reality "home" to the twentieth-century audience, who had been as bereft of history as they had been of the distinctively English mythology Tolkien so longed to realize in his own early days. As such, the style of the novel coordinates with the figure of *the* hobbit, Bilbo Baggins, a mediating presence between English modernity and the epic, northern European past who ultimately embodies the individual subject's situatedness in History.

A Silliness of Manner

As noted, *The Hobbit* was something of an accident, and even a bit of an unwelcome intruder, in Tolkien's career. Yet, without this intrusion, it is certain that his magnum opus *The Lord of the Rings* would have never been written, and it is rather unlikely that the "private and beloved nonsense," his "Silmarillion" materials, would have seen the light of day as well. Tolkien frequently mentioned the fact that each time he tried to publish this or that version of the project, he was unsuccessful, and with few exceptions, that work appeared in print only with *The Silmarillion* and other posthumous publications. As Tolkien observed, "*The Hobbit* was originally quite unconnected, though it inevitably got drawn in to the circumference of the greater construction; and in the event modified it" (*Letters* 215). Tolkien's other writing were thus affected by *The Hobbit*, even as Tolkien struggled to adjust the style of writing to fit the different forms he intended those narratives to take.

In a letter to W. H. Auden, Tolkien writes that *The Hobbit* was "unhappily meant, as far as I was concerned, as a 'children's story,' and as I had not learned sense then, and my children were not quite old enough to correct me, it has some of the silliness of manner caught unthinkingly from the kind of stuff I had had served to me" (*Letters* 215). He expresses his "deepest regret" about this, and he notes that "intelligent children" do as well. This comment indicates the degree to which *The Hobbit* initially appeared as an outlier in Tolkien's own imaginative work, not only with respect to the materials be also to their fashioning, right down to the style and manner of the presentation. It also helps to explain why the sequel, *The Lord of the Rings*, tends to be written in what most would consider a "higher" style, more like a sort of epic romance, where the narrator at times, and more so many of the main characters, tend to speak in unnaturally grandiloquent and formal manner. (The hobbits, notably, tend to speak quite plainly throughout, and Sam, as a working-class hobbit, speaks in an idiom apparently suited to his rank.) The narrator of *The Hobbit* is rather different, and even the noble characters in that novel speak relatively simply, in contemporary English, for the most part. The style of *The Hobbit* is thus a crucial aspect of its unique character, and the formal features of the prose contribute to its charms as well as its eccentricities.

Perhaps the most evident way in which the novel's "silliness of manner" appears is the frequent interpellation of the reader by the narrator, who seems to be a somewhat avuncular, familiar voice, thus positioning the reader as a sort of juvenile auditor. It is not entirely accidental that Tolkien's earliest versions of the story were literally formulated and delivered by a father reading to his own children, after all. Humphrey Carpenter, following the lead of Tolkien himself perhaps, finds these moments somewhat annoying, for he views them as tell-tale signs of a "children's story" that places severe generic and artistic restrictions of Tolkien's masterpiece. Bemoaning the "patronizing 'asides' to juvenile readers," Carpenter concedes, "it is a children's story. Despite the fact that it had been drawn into his mythology, Tolkien did not allow it to become overwhelmingly serious or even adult in tone, but stuck to his original intention of amusing his own and perhaps other people's children" (*Biography* 179, 181).

The interpellations position the reader in an imaginary space as a listener to the narrator's tale, presumably analogous to children listening to an adult in a living room somewhere, and these become persistent features of *The Hobbit*. In his essay, "Some of Tolkien's Voices," Paul Edmund Thomas observes that "[t]he narrator's tendency to speak directly to the readers is another characteristic that is not only salient but also dominant," adding, "of all the direct addresses to the readers, a count of only the most obvious ones, the ones in which the narrator refers to the readers as 'you,' comes to forty-five [...] so the full amount is actually much higher." That is, this tally would not include the many and various examples of the narrator's *assuming* a knowledge on the part of the reader, or at least the narrator's indication that such knowledge ought to be known. For example, as Tom Shippey writes, a reference to Bilbo's mother as "the *famous* Belladonna Took" implies that the author is selecting from a body of pre-existing information. Her distinction is partly explained by the theory that "one of the Took ancestors must have taken a fairy wife," immediately corrected [...] by "That was, of course, absurd." This time the word "absurd" implies that there are well-known ways of judging such statements, so well-known that the author has no need to give them, while the "of course" assumes that the reader must know these too. (*J.R.R. Tolkien*, 18–19, Shippey's emphasis)

The author or narrator thus constantly draws the reader into the world in which the story takes place.

In such commonly used rhetorical patterns as these, the reader is hailed by the author or narrator, which is arguably an "intrusive" practice. As Wayne Booth discusses in *The Rhetoric of Fiction*, such intrusions may violate Aristotle's advice in the *Poetics* (for the personal voice interferes with the role of the "poet" to imitate nature), but "it is artistically permissible to tell a story in this intrusive manner, with liberal commentary from an all-wise author," so long as the occasions in the storytelling merit these intrusions or, in other words, so long as these intrusions *work*. Booth continues: "[i]f the quality of each intrusion is not self-justifying, if the style and manner of the revealed author are not in themselves compelling, then our disbelief in this aspect of the story will hamper our enjoyment of the whole" (92, 146). Even if Tolkien later lamented the way in which the style and manner of the storytelling affected *The Hobbit*, the experience of its readers suggests that the style does in fact work, and that much of the charm of the narrative comes from the way it is presented to the reader.

This intrusive narrator also could be said to have an ideological function, and in this sense Tolkien's use of interpellation could be compared to Louis Althusser's famous reference to the concept in his "Ideology and Ideological State Apparatuses" essay. There Althusser explains that

ideology 'acts' or 'functions' in such a way that it 'recruits' subjects among the individuals (it recruits them all), or 'transforms' the individuals into subjects (it transforms them all) by that very precise operation which I have called *interpellation* or hailing, and which can be imagined along the lines of the most commonplace everyday police (or other) hailing: "Hey, you there!" (174)

The reader is established as a subject by the narrative voice in Tolkien's novel, and the reader is thus endowed with all manner of ideological and subjective character, but the overall effect is less a matter of engendering any sort of "false consciousness" (to use a somewhat old-fashioned and problematic concept) than of bringing the reader into the "world" of *The Hobbit*, of making the reader complicit in the novel's world-building. The reader is thus, like Bilbo Baggins, a part of that world system and its history even while discovering its features throughout the narrative.

As I discuss in Chapter 3, Tolkien's narrative voice somewhat mirrors and reinforces the mediatory role of Bilbo Baggins, an anachronistically modern Englishman caught up in an adventure into what appears to be an archaic past. The authoritative narrator "intrudes" into the narrative much as Bilbo "intruded" into the "Silmarillion" and related myths, legends, and histories. Additionally, by positioning the reader, juvenile or otherwise, as one seeking to gain a foothold in both "worlds"—ancient and modern, epic and novelistic, vernacular and bardic, mythic and historical, and so on—the narrative voice ultimately draws these worlds together, making visible the connections between apparently disparate epochs, lands, and ranges of experience, and thus helping to *realize* a sense of history which we are all, always and already, helping to shape, but to which we are also simultaneous subject. Like Bilbo, we are reminded that we are part of this grand narrative even as we hope to act within it and to make it better. Thus we are interpellated in the Althusserian sense, made subjects by and through ideology, but in the process come to recognize ourselves and our places within the system. Tolkien's often humorous, avuncular narrative voice thus serves as a way of disclosing to us the larger spatiotemporal structures in which we are situated.

"Praps we sits here and chats"

The narrator's voice throughout the novel sets a tone for the story, and the frequent asides or implicit addressing of the reader, although at times awkward, effectively create a mediating presence between the reader's familiar, twentieth- or twenty-first-century experience and the fantastic spaces and goings-on in the Middle-earth of Gandalf, Thorin, and Smaug. In that sense, the narrator almost doubles for Bilbo, who also serves as a mediator between modern, bourgeois English culture and the grand historical past figured forth in the characters, cultures, landscapes, and events encountered along the journey. In addition to these, Tolkien takes care to make the dialogue of the characters quite distinctive, even going so far to include approximations of crude dialects, as with the trolls' speech, or to meticulously register aspects of a character's personality in his speech, as with Gollum's distinctive speech patterns, Beorn's initially somewhat testy or impatient manner, or Smaug's intimidatingly silky voice. The diversity of voices and ways of speaking within *The Hobbit* help to round out and supply realistic detail to a fantastic world, while also serving as reminders of the connection between this fantastic history and our present situation.

The opening chapter highlights distinctive ways of speaking, occasionally also foregrounding the artificial and formal nature of our verbal interactions, often to comical effect. Gandalf's delightful observations about the many meanings of the phrase *Good morning* tips the reader off, and we know that Tolkien's passion for storytelling is closely related to his passion for the *words* with which stories are told. Some of the jokes are literally embedded in the words themselves. For example, as Shippey observes, Bilbo Baggins lives in a place called Bag-End, which is a literal English translation of the phrase *cul-de-sac*, a term that even the French do not normally use for such an *impasse* or *dead-end* in roads. Rather, the word *cul-de-sac* "has its origins in snobbery"; the term "is accordingly a peculiarly ridiculous piece of English class-feeling—and Bag-End a defiantly English reaction to it" (*Road* 71). In his own stuffy, bourgeois Englishness, exemplified in part by how he "good-morninged" Gandalf (5), Bilbo seems suited to home on a *cul-de-sac*, but one referred to as Bag-End.

Along those lines, Bilbo likes to quote his father, whom we had been told throughout the novel represents the sensible, unadventurous "Baggins side" of the hobbit's personality. If Bilbo has his mother's Tookish side to thank for his spirit of wonder, he nevertheless relies on his father's pragmatic sayings (or banal clichés) at crucial moments of danger, notably, when he is mustering up the courage to face the dragon. In his first foray into the dragon's lair, Bilbo expresses annoyance that the dwarves intend to make him perform this perilous task alone, after he had saved them twice already, but he reasons "'third time pays for all' as my father used to say" (212). On his second visit to the dragon, Bilbo notes "'Every worm has his weak spot,' as my father used to say, though I am sure it was not from personal experience" (221), and later he assures the dwarves, "'Where there's life there's hope!' as my father used to say, and 'Third time pays for all'" (235). That Bilbo relies on such sayings in these dangerous moments speaks to Tolkien's views on simple, ordinary, middle-class English folk "wisdom."

Also notable is the foregrounding of the very formal, patently artificial language used by those in powerful positions, as opposed to the straightforward vernacular of regular folks. Thorin, for example, when making a speech—as he does on several occasions in the novel—tends to a manner that is quite verbose, long-winded, and recognizably close to the rhetorical bluster of the politician. After beginning such an address during the "unexpected party," the narrator intercedes, explaining "This was Thorin's style. He was an important dwarf. If he had been allowed, he would probably have gone on like this until he was out of breath, without telling any one there anything that was not known already" (17). Much later, when they are entering the Lonely Mountain, the narrator again interrupts what looks to be a windy oration by addressing the reader directly: "You are familiar with Thorin's style on important occasions, so I will not give you any more of it, though he went on for a good deal longer than this" (212). Thus does Tolkien's narrator gently criticize a certain form of political discourse, favoring what might be considered the plain speech of Bilbo and others of middle-class temperament.

Tolkien also registers this skepticism with respect to the speech of the powerful when depicting an actual politician, the elected Master of Lake-town. The Master is a slightly villainous character, and we learn at the very end of the novel that he had come to a bad end after embezzling the town's gold. However, he is not so much evil as canny, calculating, and hypocritical, but his skills at swaying public opinion through speech are acknowledged. For instance, after we witness a brief oration delivered to the townspeople, the narrator adds, "As you can see, the Master had not got his position for nothing" (253). As with "the voice of Saruman" in

The Lord of the Rings, which seemed almost like enchantment involving actual magic, Tolkien here indicates and bemoans the power of words effectively used by authorities to sway public opinion. As Tolkien put it, "Saruman's voice was not hypnotic but persuasive. Those who listened were not in danger of falling into a trance, but of agreeing with his arguments" (*Letters* 276–277). Of course, embedded within the critique of the rhetoric of politician lies another, the critique of the gullibility of the masses who listen.

If the narrative voice seems to favor plain, middle-class speech and is skeptical of the discourse of the powerful, the depiction of lower-class discourse also implies value judgments. Specifically, the trolls—who are given common English names, William (also called Bill Huggins), Bert, and Tom—are made to speak with an accent likely associated with uneducated, rustic types. For instance, when Bilbo is caught ("copped") by William, another troll asks what "it" is, and William answers, "Lumme, if I knows! What are yer?" (36), and the trolls' dialogue runs along similarly vernacular lines throughout. "They were trolls. Obviously trolls," recognizable for "their size, and the shape of their legs, not to mention their language, which was not drawing-room fashion, at all" (34). The dialect used by Tolkien accentuates the rudeness and crudeness of the speakers. Trolls are not allegorical figures of the working class, of course, but by depicting them as uncultured rubes, even more so than as the terrifying monsters they also clearly are, *The Hobbit* invites the comparison. The goblins of the Misty Mountains speak more eloquently, as with the Great Goblin's interrogation of Thorin, but then they are not really allowed to speak as much, as they are killed as quickly and as numerously as possible. Other "enemies," such as the spiders in Mirkwood, also seem to have lower-class modes of speaking (e.g. "kill'em now and hang'em dead" or "I saw one a-struggling just now" [157]), and even the wargs' language, which is understood by Gandalf alone among the company, sounds to Bilbo "terrible [...] as if all their talk was about cruel and wicked things, as it was" (101). Of the monsters, only the aristocratic-seeming Smaug proves to be a supremely gifted rhetorician, with "rather an overwhelming personality," and we learn that "dragon-talk" can have adverse effects on the "inexperienced" auditor. Perhaps this is similar to the warning about politicians' speech.

Of course, the most exceptional and memorable voice within *The Hobbit* belongs to Gollum, a creature named for the non-verbal, unintentional vocalization he periodically makes when speaking. Even though Gollum's physical stature and personal interactions with Bilbo changed dramatically between the first and second editions of the novel (in order to make the ring more consistent with the artifact as it appears in *The Lord of the Rings*), it is striking that Gollum's style of speech, and the riddles used in the competition, did not change. Gollum's speech is the most distinctive of all, as with his first utterance upon seeing Bilbo: "Bless us and splash us, my precioussss! I guess it's a choice feast, at least a tasty morsel it'd make us, Gollum!" (72). As Shippey has pointed out, this is the only time in *The Hobbit* that Gollum uses the pronoun "I"; as it happens, Gollum also never says "you." As Shippey observes, it was Tolkien's "brilliant" idea "to mark Gollum out by his strange use of pronouns. [...] Gollum's consistent verbal oddity gives a distinctive personality, or lack of one, which is entirely original" (*J.R.R. Tolkien* 30).

The narrator informs us that Gollum "always called himself 'my precious'" and "always spoke to himself through never having anyone else to speak to" (72). Although Tolkien originally may not have had anything else in mind when he made Gollum speak this way, the loss of a sense of individuated "self" fits nicely with the subsequent vision of the One Ring, whose power can cause the ringbearer's own person to "fade," as exemplified by the fate of the Ringwraiths of *The Lord of the Rings*. Although Gollum in *The Hobbit* remains mostly the same, in the sequel he is shown to be torn between the Sméagol he was and the Gollum he had become. Among other scholars, Jane Chance has observed that "Sméagol tends to speak in complete sentences, using the first-person [singular] pronoun," unlike Gollum ("Subversive" 157). But even in the earlier, less vivid portrait of Gollum, one could argue that the effacing of selfhood might be an effect of the prolonged isolation and solitude. If nothing else, Gollum seems eager to engage Bilbo in conversation, and not merely to eat him.

The potential separation along the lines of social class may also be a factor. The drawing out of and addition of *ess* sounds indicates a sort of reptilian hissing, but the discourse itself seems to be of the same, simple working-class diction, as with the use of "praps" for *perhaps*: "Praps we sits here and chats with it a bitsy, my preciousss. It likes riddles, praps it does, does it?" (73). The troll Bert had also said "P'raps," but there the apostrophe indicates an elision, whereas with Gollum it seems to be, as with the added *esses*, simply the language he uses. Gollum's diction places him in a subordinate role among the class hierarchies of Middle-earth, even if he is a unique figure within that world. As Yvette Kisor and others have pointed out, Gollum's discourse seems somewhat infantile, a form of "baby talk" (160), which may be another way in which Gollum is positioned as subordinate to others. However, this feature arguably adds to the sense of horror as well, given the uncanny disjunction between the "argot of the nursery" (Rosebury 81) and the cannibalistic menace facing Bilbo during the riddle game.

Of all the voices in *The Hobbit*, a novel which features so many different characters and different modes of speaking, Gollum's stands out. It may be the case that, as Tolkien has written in "Of Fairy-Stories," "the dragon had the trade-mark *Of Faërie* written plain upon him" and "[i]n whatever world he had his being it was an Otherworld" (135), but in the minds of many readers, Gollum might be Middle-earth's most memorable "monster." In this sense, the most haunting moment of the entire novel may be when Gollum, filled in equal parts with "hatred and despair," utters the memorable *cri-de-coeur*: "Thief, thief, thief! Baggins! We hates it, we hates it, we hates it for ever!" (87).

From a Mythic to a Historical Mode

Tolkien's style in *The Hobbit*, particular in its distinctiveness from that of his other writings, owes something to the genre. His earlier work on the "Silmarillion" materials was very much informed by an epic tradition in which a sort of bardic narrator, having invoked the Muse, delivers the narrative in a more or less uniform manner. The narrator of the *Kalevala*, for example, is not going to make humorous asides to the reader. But the narrators of *Don Quixote*, *Tristram Shandy*, or *Moby-Dick* do not hesitate to address the reader *quâ* reader relatively frequently, nor do their presentations of various characters' voices demonstrate any kind of standard manner of speech across social classes. The novel as a literary form, in terms made well known by Mikhail Bakhtin in *The Dialogic Imagination*, is both multiformal and heteroglossic. The style of *The Hobbit*, in part, comports with its form as a novel, the first novel Tolkien ever wrote, and depending on your definition, arguably the only one he ever wrote. (That is, some might consider *The Lord of the Rings* to be different from the novel, perhaps more like the "modern epic" as Franco Moretti has characterized that form.) The novelistic character of *The Hobbit* also makes visible the shift in Tolkien's work from the mythic to the historical register.

Tolkien's writing manifestly, though perhaps unconsciously, puts into play multiple generic modes and characteristics, arguably establishing a hybrid form, a palimpsest in which layers of mythic, epic, romantic, pastoral, realist, and modernist forms coexist and infuse one another, as the overall historical and geographical world system of Middle-earth unfurls itself before the reader's eyes. By the mid-1930s Tolkien's "private and beloved nonsense" was forced to move "from myth to history" with the advent and incorporation of hobbits. As Dimitra Fimi notes, "[w]ith *The Hobbit*, some elements of his legendarium became fixed because they were published and therefore available to the public as authoritative facts from the author" (120). This concerned Tolkien enough that he spent much of his later life making notes and revising drafts in an effort "to reconcile certain of these 'facts' with his original conception of the mythology or with its changing nature" (120). *The Hobbit* itself, in Fimi's words, is a "hybrid story," which started as an independent tale invented for his own children and later became connected to the larger, mythic "Silmarillion" *legendarium*. As such, when published, the novel is "a mishmash of northern folkloric elements, Germanic nomenclature, and scripts as well as new original 'inventions,'" such as "[t]he 'newfangled' hobbits and Gollum," which "verged on the comic in comparison with the tragic and heroic characters of his mythology" (118, 119). *The Hobbit* is thus a major turning point in Tolkien's career, in many different respects, but it also marks what Fimi refers to as "the shift in his creative writing from a 'mythical' to a 'historical' mode" (120).

Tolkien had been (and continued to be) deeply committed to the project of "myth-making," for he viewed the making of myths is not an evasion from the scientific apperception of the ways this world works, but a necessary complement to it. In Tolkien's theory of Sub-Creation, for instance, the "secondary world" created by the human artist is an imitation of the "primary world" (i.e., God's own Creation), which means that all myth or fantasy partake of that "real" world. But the novel form changed the approach. "*The Hobbit* gave birth to *The Lord of the Rings* and inaugurated a new way of writing. Tolkien was not writing mythology anymore, he was writing a novel" (Fimi 119). Although Tolkien had begun to experiment with the novel as a means for telling his "Silmarillion" stories as early as *The Lost Road* in his drafts from the 1920s, it was not until *The Hobbit* that he wrote a complete novel. Earlier, he had been able to adjust, modify, revise, and generally tinker with his mythological elements in various ways, but *The Hobbit* and the demand for its sequel changed everything, requiring Tolkien to set down a clearer history and arguably more "realistic" world for his narrative. This also helps to account for the increasing prominence of humans or human-like hobbits, instead of elves, in the larger story that makes up the Saga of the Jewels and the Rings, which is how he had hoped to present an integrated version of the "Silmarillion" and *The Lord of the Rings*.

By the time he writes *The Lord of the Rings*, Tolkien had managed to square the circle of the myth-*versus*-history conundrum within his writings by using an ingenious device: "The Red Book of Westmarch." Tolkien establishes as a regnant conceit within the world of his narratives that Bilbo Baggins himself, while living in Rivendell, had translated the many stories and legends that are part of the "Silmarillion" from the original elvish languages, and we learn that the stories we had been reading are merely the translation into English of parts of the "Red Book," translations performed by an Oxford University professor named J. R. R. Tolkien. As Fimi concludes,

> [t]he choice of the "Red Book" as the method of transmission of the legendarium to the readers in modern times was a nearly perfect solution: Bilbo would have had access to the records of Rivendell where much material from Númenor was also preserved. The mythology would not reach us directly through the Elves, but through the Númenorians and the subsequent "mediation" of the hobbits. (128)

Hobbits, already an anachronistic feature of Tolkien's world, are thus superbly suited to help to bridge the vast mythic and historical gap, bringing the story from a distant age into our own present.

This marvelously effective framing device allows for a rather "realistic" transition from the mythical world of the "Silmarillion," the legends of which would have largely been set down in *lays*, ballads, lyric poetry, and especially in the form of the epic, to the more straightforwardly historical world of humans (i.e., *our* world), for whom the heteroglossic and multi-formal novel becomes the predominant modern representative literary form. *The Hobbit* itself, in retrospect, exemplifies the process whereby Tolkien made the move from myth to history and from epic to novel, for Bilbo's "intrusion" represents the interventions of the most prosaic yet profound aspects of history into a grandly poetic and mythic fantasy world. In this way, the very style of *The Hobbit* helps to realize what will become Tolkien's larger political and philosophical project of making history meaningfully accessible to modern readers who are increasingly unconscious of both the past and its connections to themselves. As a historical novel, *The Hobbit* uses fantasy as a means of making the historical register all the more meaningful and "real" to its readers.

3

Nasty Disturbing Uncomfortable Things: The Intrusions of History

"Men make their own history," as Karl Marx writes in *The Eighteenth Brumaire*, "but they do not make it as they please; they do not make it under self-selected circumstances, but under circumstances existing already, given and transmitted from the past. The tradition of all dead generations weighs like a nightmare on the brains of the living" (15). This characteristically poetic formulation gets at the heart of a historical truth equally valid for Tolkien as for the Marxist tradition: we as individual and collective subjects do indeed make history, yet we are also subject to historical forces beyond our control. *The Hobbit* is, in part, a story about an ordinary person who "makes history," but it is also very much a tale about history, about our situatedness in history, and about the emergence of a historical consciousness.

Indeed, *The Hobbit* is arguably a "historical novel," which is bound to sound rather strange, given that it is such a canonical work of fantasy, a genre sometimes thought to be inimical to, or at least separated from, the "real world" and its history. To be sure, especially with respect to what has come to be regarded as Tolkienesque fantasy, there is a strong historical element, and European medievalism in particular has been established

© The Author(s), under exclusive license to Springer Nature
Switzerland AG 2022
R. T. Tally Jr., *J. R. R. Tolkien's* The Hobbit,
Palgrave Science Fiction and Fantasy: A New Canon,
https://doi.org/10.1007/978-3-031-11266-9_3

as an all-too-fertile territory on which to develop tales of swords and sorcery. Part of the allure of the fantastic stems from its otherworldliness, but such alterity can be found also in that element of time-travel, of visiting a distant past version of "our world," now made unfamiliar by the span of the ages and its effects. Thus, for instance, Tolkien insisted that the label *Middle-earth* referred, not to a distinctively imaginary place (such as C.S. Lewis's Narnia, L. Frank Baum's Oz, or the Alice's Wonderland of Lewis Carroll), but to our own very "real" world, only a version of it with a different history. Responding to a largely favorable review of *The Return of the King*, written by W. H. Auden in 1956, Tolkien explained,

> I am historically minded. Middle-earth is not an imaginary world. The name is the modern form (appearing in the 13th century and still in use) of *midden-erd > middel-erd*, an ancient name for the *oikoumenē*, the abiding place of Men, the objectively real world, in use specifically opposed to imaginary worlds (as Fairyland) or unseen worlds (as Heaven or Hell). The theatre of my tale is this earth, the one in which we now live, but the historical period is imaginary. The essentials of that abiding place are all there (at any rate for inhabitants of N.W. Europe), so naturally it feels familiar, even if a little glorified by the enchantment of distance in time. (*Letters* 239)

As if to underscore this point more definitively, Tolkien ends the long note by repeating it: "Mine is not an 'imaginary' world, but an imaginary historical moment on 'Middle-earth'—which is our habitation" (244).

Needless to say, one hopes, Tolkien's position on this matter ought not be taken too literally. For instance, the maps included in *The Hobbit*, *The Lord of the Rings*, and *The Silmarillion* are not expected to align with the geography of Europe, even if some have tried to do so. (In what must be a fun coincidence for fans of *Dracula*, one map overlay developed by UCLA geography professor Peter Bird locates The Shire in England's West Midlands and shows Mordor to be roughly in the position of Transylvania.) The *oikounemē* that is Middle-earth is the world we live in, but that does not mean that the physical geography, no more than the political geography, needs to be aligned with that of actually existing Europe or other parts of the planet. Tolkien's point is not to make readers seek out the "real places" in which his fictional tales are set (*pace* John Garth's *The Worlds of J.R.R. Tolkien*, which purports to uncover "the places that inspired Middle-earth"), but to think of the ways that we are part of the larger narrative of this world's history.

Among other things, *The Hobbit* tells the tale of an adventure, but beyond the details of Bilbo's travels, the encounters along the way, and the events in which he takes part, it is also a story of his coming into historical consciousness. In its opening scene, the wizard Gandalf tells Bilbo Baggins, "I am looking for someone to share an adventure I am arranging, and it's very difficult to find anyone," to which the hobbit responds, "I should think so—in these parts! We are plain quiet folks and have no use for adventures. Nasty disturbing uncomfortable things! Make you late for dinner! I can't think what anybody sees in them" (4). The intrusion of this adventure upon Bilbo's "plain, quiet" life opens up a world to him in which his own actions make history, while also recognizing the degree to which he had unwittingly been subject to history all along.

A Waverley of the Shire

The modern fantasy novel, of which *The Hobbit* might be considered an exemplar, would appear as nearly the opposite of the historical novel, a genre that developed through an admixture of romance and realism to establish a firm location, in time and space, visible in the historical events of the "real world." Fantasy, it is usually assumed, deals with imaginary worlds quite distant and distinct from the real one, and some fantastic works present places somewhat out of time, akin perhaps to a recognizably historical moment in our world, but not *of* the world. Perhaps unwittingly, in *The Hobbit*, Tolkien managed to establish many of the parameters of conventional fantasy, amounting to what Terry Pratchett has half-jokingly referred to as the "consensus fantasy universe" ("Why Gandalf Never Married"). But, at the same time, *The Hobbit* engenders a historical reality in a novel only apparently outside of history, depicting an otherworld that is altogether worldly.

In traditional literary history, Sir Walter Scott is frequently credited with inventing the genre of the historical novel, with *Waverley, or, 'Tis Sixty Years Since* published in 1814. *Waverley* focused on a rather unremarkable English aristocrat who finds himself caught up among the opposing sides of the Jacobite Rebellion in Scotland, and thus like Bilbo in his own world, Edward Waverley suddenly becomes a participant in the historic conflicts of his age. Indeed, *The Hobbit* could be read in the context of Georg Lukács's magnificent study, *The Historical Novel*, in which an ordinary or "maintaining" individual sustains a representation of world-historical events and individuals that discloses the emerging historical consciousness. The form of the novel, *The Hobbit*, incorporates and transcends the traditionally fantastic content, making its otherworldliness all the more critical to a figurative mapping of the "real" world. *The Hobbit* is an especially good point of entry into such a complicated world system, since the anachronistic intermediary that is Bilbo allows readers to see that world from the perspective of one who is nearly as unfamiliar with it as we are.

Bilbo Baggins is an obvious anachronism, who seems almost to time-travel in his movement eastward from the comfortable and familiar landscape of the Shire toward not only Lake-town and the Lonely Mountain, but to the historic events that occur in and are represented by those faraway places. Apart from certain distinctively "hobbitic" characteristics, like woolly toes and uncanny stealth, Bilbo is clearly a late-Victorian or Edwardian bourgeois Englishman, a modern if still somewhat traditional inhabitant of a bucolic place not unlike the West Midlands of Tolkien's youth. A "very well-to-do hobbit," as noted on the first page of the novel, Bilbo is presumably a relatively inoffensive member of a *rentier* class who neither plies a trade or employs others to work for him. (In *The Lord of the Rings*, we learn that Hamfast "The Gaffer" Gamgee served as the Baggins's gardener, a role taken over in Frodo's day by his son Samwise.) Although Bilbo has taken the occasional interest in the world beyond his region, owing in large part to an adventurous streak inherited from his mother's side of the family, as well as his love of maps, Bilbo knows quite little, practically or theoretically, about that world. To name but one of the almost innumerable examples of his ignorance or naïveté that readers encounter in the narrative, Bilbo "was not good at skinning rabbits or cutting up meat, being used to having it delivered by the butcher all ready to cook" (*Hobbit* 110). What could be more quotidian than purchasing food from a butcher? And yet, in that scene, Bilbo dines on rabbit-meat prepared by dwarves that had been delivered by giant eagles after being rescued from hordes of goblins and wolves, which is already quite an adventure tale to tell.

Tolkien managed to sneak into the novel elements of his earlier mythological world, including references to Gondolin, the "Goblin Wars," and even Sauron himself (presented as "the Necromancer"). But, particularly as he attempted to integrate the narrative of *The Hobbit* into the wider cosmos of his imagined Middle-earth, Tolkien regretted some of the choices he had made. For example, Tolkien was not happy with his use of "conventional and inconsistent Grimm's fairy-tale dwarves" in the novel (*Letters* 26), who worked relatively well for a comic tale of a hobbit, but did not fit neatly within a world containing a Nargothrond or Khazad-dûm. Still, in Thorin's august company, Bilbo is the fish that finds himself "out of water," thereby acquiring "an inkling of water" (*Letters* 64). This metaphor works effectively and captures an individual's realization of his or her place in a larger history, whether that be Bilbo in the caverns beneath the Misty Mountains or readers situated in their own place and time within a vast, spatiotemporal system. Bilbo's befuddlement signals his dawning sense of understanding, which in turn grants readers an entrée into this world.

This is also an apt metaphor for history itself, of which Bilbo and we all are a part, but which brings itself into the open mostly just when it becomes uncomfortable. As Fredric Jameson famously remarked, "History is what hurts, it is what refuses desire and sets inexorable limits to individual as well as collective praxis, which its 'ruses' turn into grisly and ironic reversals of their overt intention" (*Political Unconscious* 102). But in the relative discomfort or unfamiliarity it brings, history is, perhaps paradoxically, similar to fantasy. For instance, as Jerome de Groot has noted in his study of the historical novel, "History is other, and the present familiar. The historian's job is often to explain the transition between these states. The historical novelist similarly explores the dissonance and displacement between then and now, making the past recognizable but simultaneously authentically familiar" (3). The same might be said for fantasy, which often presents a world radically different from our own, and yet makes it seem not only possible, but actually real, at least within its sphere. In *The Hobbit*, to be sure, dragons are remote, otherworldly, and the stuff of legend or myth; and yet, Smaug is all too real, and the experience of traveling alongside Bilbo, Gandalf, and the dwarves, is for the duration of the narrative an utterly real, perhaps historical, experience. In accompanying Bilbo especially, we discern his own awakening of historical perspective, moving from the good-natured but impatient hobbit who "Good mornings" Gandalf in the first chapter of *The Hobbit* to the "hero," as Gandalf names him in the Council of Elrond scene of *The Lord of the Rings*, whose accidental discovery of the One Ring will become quite possibly the most significant, or *historic*, event of the age.

In Lukács's analysis of the historical novel as a literary form, one of the key, defining characteristics of the genre is the foregrounded presence of the ordinary little guy, someone against whom the Hegelian "world-historical individual," such as a Cromwell or Napoleon, stands out in the distance. In *The Hobbit*, Bilbo's position is like that of Waverley, an utterly unremarkable, apparently insignificant figure, who stumbles into the great world-historical events of the epoch and takes part in them. As Lukács writes of Scott's protagonists, and he could as just as easily be thinking of a Bilbo Baggins type of character,

> The "hero" of a Scott novel is always a more or less mediocre, average English gentleman. He generally possesses a certain, though never outstanding, degree of practical intelligence, a certain moral fortitude and decency which even rises to a capacity for self-sacrifice, but which never grows into a sweeping human passion, is never the enraptured devotion to a great cause. [...] That he builds his novels around a "middling," merely correct and never heroic "hero" is the clearest proof of Scott's exceptional and revolutionary epic gifts. (*Historical Novel* 33)

The fact that Middle-earth is not "real" in the same sense that Waverly's Scotland is real is beside the point, and in any case does not bear directly on the form of the literary work. Within the novel, each place is as real as the other.

Tolkien's commitment to the creation, or "sub-creation," of a world apart does not necessarily mean that Tolkien turns away from an engagement with the real world. The imaginary projection of an alternate reality in Middle-earth, with its seemingly integrated or "closed" *Lebenstotalität*—which, according to Lukács in *The Theory of the Novel* characterizes the age and the world of the epic—figures forth a kind of truth not seen in more crudely allegorical narratives. In "On Fairy-Stories," Tolkien insists that "creative Fantasy is founded upon the hard recognition that things are so in the world as it appears under the sun; on a recognition of fact, but not a slavery to it" (144). Moreover, as Tolkien points out, the "perilous realm" of Faërie "contains many things besides elves and fays, and besides dwarfs, witches, trolls, giants, or dragons: it holds the seas, the sun, the moon, the sky; and the earth, and all things that are in it: tree and bird, water and stone, wine and bread, and ourselves, mortal men, when we are enchanted" (113). In other words, even in their apparent otherworldliness and amid the mythic elements included in their overall substance, these tales are worldly and historical.

The Bilbo who returns to the Shire is, as Gandalf notes, not the same person as the one who left it: he is part of a global history and, more importantly, he is aware of it. Henceforth, his interactions with elves or dwarves are not isolated encounters with creatures from a mist-enveloped, legendary past, a region that might as well be a fantastic otherworld, but are woven into a spatiotemporal continuum that includes Bilbo and his kin, along with kings and counselors, gods and monsters. But Bilbo also remains the happy-go-lucky creature who, when reminded by Gandalf that he is "quite a little fellow in a wide world," can declare "Thank goodness!" as he passes the tobacco-jar. A fittingly ordinary ending to a historical novel.

The Vanishing Mediator; or, the Uses of Anachronism

The Hobbit, as everyone knows, is marked by anachronism. Its titular hero is a sort of fantastic being, who is not quite the same as a human while also being about as anthropomorphic as can be imagined. (Hence, hobbits are generally thought of as a race distinct from men, elves, dwarves, and others, but Tolkien also indicates that they are fundamentally human, just diminutive with respect to "the Big People, as they call us" [*Hobbit* 2].) Yet Bilbo also quite clearly an Englishman, and his love of comfort, including his enjoyment of the anachronistic tobacco (a term which was judiciously replaced with *pipe-weed* in the sequel), along with other mannerisms, marks him as a typical bourgeois of the early twentieth century. As the novel begins, Bilbo has relatively little knowledge of history and some interest in myth, but then history and myth, in the guise of Gandalf, Thorin, and the dwarves, literally come knocking at his door, entreating him to venture forth from his present, quasi-Edwardian existence into the depths of time and space beyond. Bilbo's anachronism, which is played for laughs in parts of the narrative and highlights his role as a "fish out of water," is actually a crucial element of *The Hobbit*'s and Tolkien's historical project.

As I have said, Tolkien later regretted many of the anachronisms of *The Hobbit*, particularly when he was trying to harmonize the stories and styles of that novel and *The Lord of the Rings*, yet even these apparent "errors" in the overall world-building of Tolkien's universe have their unforeseen advantages. For instance, in *The Historical Novel*, Lukács notes that the apparently realist text includes "necessary anachronisms" that help to enable it to, as it were, step outside of itself and present something like a social totality (61). Additionally, much as Tolkien may have wished he had not included references to golf, football, or tobacco in *The Hobbit* (he did manage to change *tomatoes*, a word of Aztec origin, to *pickles* in the second edition, but it is not clear that he did so because it was anachronistic [see Rateliff 784]), and much as he endeavored to avoid such linguistic and other anachronisms in *The Lord of the Rings*, the "estrangement effect" of such jarring moments, as Brecht might have noted, does recall the reader to the historicity and historical situation of the narrative, which is yet another way of "realizing" history within the seamless web of story.

Tolkien recognizes and emphasizes the distinction between myth and history, as when he points out that the One Ring (in *The Lord of the Rings*) is "a mythical feature, even though the world of the tales is conceived in more or less historical terms," for example (*Letters* 279).

However, like Lukács and Jameson, Tolkien also understands the degree to which they overlap or rather imbue one another with their respective powers in the form of narrative, which is to say, in the way the humans make sense of and give form to the world. Tolkien observes that "History often resembles 'Myth,' because they are both ultimately of the same stuff" ("On Fairy-Stories" 127). That is, even if the mythical characters or events did not exist in the "real world," some account of the nameless persons they are made to represent is nevertheless thrown into what Tolkien refers to as "the Cauldron of Story." In that cauldron, "where so many potent things lie simmering agelong on the fire," "the great figures of Myth and History" emerge, and the forms that their narratives take will depend on the mythmaker, the historian, or, more simply, the storyteller (127–128). Moreover, Tolkien adds, "if we speak of a Cauldron, we must not wholly forget the Cooks. There are many things in the Cauldron, but the Cooks do not dip in the ladle quite blindly. Their selection is important" (128). In *The Hobbit*, enchantments are to be found less in magic per se than in stories, tales well crafted and well told. "Small wonder that *spell* means both a story told, and a formula of power over living men" (Tolkien, "On Fairy-Stories" 128).

But *modern* fantasy, of the type that *The Hobbit* and *The Lord of the Rings* represents, also brings the modern novel and its conventions to bear on the medieval and otherworldly raw materials, in such a way as to draw readers in and keep them entertained. The lack of some of these elements, and of hobbits in particular, may be have cost *The Silmarillion* in the long run; Tolkien himself acknowledged that the lack of hobbits would affect the "appeal" of the "Silmarillion" (see *Letters* 238).

Along those lines, Shippey has identified two key problems that *The Silmarillion* presents, which may help to explain why Tolkien never satisfactorily completed the nearly sixty-year project and why a number of readers find *The Silmarillion* as published so more difficult and less enjoyable than *The Lord of the Rings*. First, without the hobbits, there is a lack of a mediator; for example, "Bilbo acts as the link between modern times and the archaic world of dwarves and dragons," which makes exploring the world of *The Silmarillion*, but also experiencing it in its full verisimilitude, more difficult for the reader. Second, by filling in the historical *lacunae* implied but not expressed in *The Hobbit* and *The Lord of the Rings*, the "Silmarillion" materials lacked the desirable silences or omissions that provided the "impression of depth" or the "illusion of historical truth" which makes the fantasy world so enchanted, precisely because it also makes it so seemingly "real" (Shippey, *Road* 228–229). This is a crucial factor for Tolkien, who spoke of the importance of "untold stories." In a wartime letter to Christopher, Tolkien refers to Celebrimbor, the elf craftsman who had fashioned the three rings for the elven kings, but also a very distant and arguably minor figure who plays no part in the events of *The Lord of the Rings*, and says,

> A story must be told or there'll be no story, yet it is the untold stories that are most moving. I think you are moved by *Celebrimbor* because it conveys a sudden sense of endless *untold* stories: mountains seen far away, never to be climbed, distant trees (like Niggle's) never to be approached. (*Letters* 110–111)

Tolkien's reference here to "Leaf by Niggle," a tale of an artist who attempts to paint a tree, but manages to successfully paint just one leaf beautifully, is all the more meaningful in the context of Tolkien's career. "Leaf by Niggle" is understandably taken to be an allegorical representation of Tolkien's own struggles to complete the "Silmarillion" or the Saga of the Jewels and the Rings, of which, perhaps, *The Lord of the Rings* is merely one marvelously realized "leaf." Nevertheless, that novel benefits immensely from the "untold stories" that enrich its historical and geographical scope. In *The Silmarillion* itself, as Shippey suggests, the detailed "telling" of such untold stories ultimately undermines it own powers of enchantment for many readers.

Living in a world in which Gondolin or the Goblin Wars are background realities, but not described in detail, Bilbo serves as a mediator between the modern reader and the dense, deep history that he finds himself bound up in. The desire for a mediator is not just a matter of fantasy, a genre that in fact presents rather few problems in this regard. Readers have no trouble understanding dragons, after all. What may be harder to *realize* is the world in which that dragon operates, the complex and rich historical web that turns the Kingdom under the Mountain, the Lake-town, the elves of Mirkwood, the goblins of Gundabad, and such other distinctive places and cultures into the meaningful references that they are. This in turn gives the narrative of the adventures of Bilbo in the present its real urgency and vitality. Tolkien is rightly best known for his "world-building," a term that includes both history and geography (of which I have more to say in Chapters 4 and 5), but part of what makes his world so vivid is the mediating role played by hobbits. Tolkien himself saw "the value of Hobbits" primarily "in putting earth under the feet of 'romance'" (*Letters* 215). Bilbo, for all the outlandishness (literally!) on display for much of the narrative, provides the bridge between quotidian English modernity and an exotic, otherworldly past.

Shippey has discussed the "two sides" of *The Hobbit* in terms of this anachronistic divide: "on the one side, there is the modern middle-class English Bilbo, on the other the archaic world which lies behind both vulgar folk-tale and its aristocratic, indeed heroic ancestors" (*J.R.R. Tolkien* 18). Bilbo's fussiness and the variously out-of-place items and references (e.g., clocks, pocket-handkerchiefs, etc.) highlight the differences between the two registers. Shippey goes on to note that,

> the two side are going to clash, and much of *The Hobbit* is about the clash of styles, attitudes, behaviour patterns—though in the end one might conclude that they are not as far apart as they first seemed, and that Bilbo has just as much right to the archaic world and its treasures as Thorin or Bard. (18)

If Bilbo has a right to this world into which he so awkwardly finds himself thrust, it is because he comes to realize that it is also *his* world, that he is *of* it, and that his earlier sense of separation from the tides of time and the reaches of space was false. Similarly, though this is not Shippey's point, Thorin and Bard are *of* the modern world, since their participation in making its history shaped modern forms and contents as well. *The Hobbit*'s oddly anachronistic features thus serve to make visible and make real the interconnectedness and totality of history.

Bilbo not only has a mediatory role, but we might say, at the risk of sounding cheeky, that he is a sort of "vanishing mediator," in the sense used by Jameson. (Yes, of course, Bilbo also possesses a ring that bestows the power of invisibility, so he might be thought of as a mediator who frequently "vanishes" in another sense.) In a well-known essay on Max Weber, Jameson introduces the idea of the vanishing mediator as "a catalytic agent that permits an exchange of energy between two otherwise mutually exclusive terms" ("Vanishing" 331). That is, the mediator is a necessary component of the transition of one phase to the next, making possible, or making visible, the new state of affairs, before itself receding, "vanishing," or in any event becoming no longer a crucial element in the historical equation. In the case of Bilbo, the character on whom the narrative is almost entirely focalized, his mediation is necessary for the reader to make sense of the world of Middle-earth presented in *The Hobbit*, but by the end, the world has so well understood as to become almost familiar. *The Lord of the Rings* will introduce a wealth of new information about that world, its history, its places, and its cultures—indeed, after leaving Rivendell, that novel never again, until the final chapters, depicts its various protagonists in the northern regions in which the entirety of *The Hobbit* takes place—but all of that will be somewhat cognizable thanks to Bilbo's prior adventures. At any rate, while they still have a mediatory role to play, Frodo and the other hobbits of *The Lord of the Rings*, including Bilbo of course, are no longer necessary in the same way, and Bilbo can recede into the contours of the world, becoming just another (major) character we encounter along the way.

As I mentioned in Chapter 2, the distinctive narrative voice used by Tolkien in *The Hobbit* also functions in a mediatory way. The "knowing author," interpellating the reader frequently, implicitly includes the reader in the world even though, in reality, all of this ought to be new to the audience. "There is a kind of unfairness in it, for the author naturally knows everything and the reader nothing about the world being introduced," observes Shippey, "but the voice assumes a kind of complicity, and every time another piece of the picture is being filled in, another part of the mental map is disclosed" (*J.R.R. Tolkien* 20). The narrative voice mediates between the modern and ancient worlds, as does Bilbo's anachronistic character, but also envelops the reader (again, like Bilbo) in a world that gradually, and indeed quite quickly, becomes so familiar as to be recognized as our own. We know that Belladonna Took is already "famous" as soon as the narrator mentions "the famous Belladonna Took," just as we know that trolls turn to stone when exposed to daylight or we know the way to talk to dragons when the time comes for us to know such things. In a way, then, we could say that Bilbo's historical narrative, along with the manner in which it is presented, brings Middle-earth into being as a cognizable totality, one in which his and others' stories can "seamlessly" intertwine.

The Seamless Web of Story

As noted before, at the very end of *The Hobbit* there is a scene that takes place "some years" after Bilbo has returned from his adventure, when Gandalf and Balin visit him in his home at Bag-End. Hearing the news of Lake-town's prosperity (i.e., people there are saying that "the rivers run with gold"), Bilbo says, "Then the prophecies of the old songs have turned out to be true, after a fashion!" Gandalf responds:

> Of course! […] And why should not they prove true? Surely you don't disbelieve the prophecies, because you had a hand in bringing them about yourself? You don't really suppose, do you, that all your adventures and escapes were managed by mere luck, just for your sole benefit? You are a very fine person, Mr. Baggins, and I am very fond of you, but you are really only quite a little fellow in a wide world after all! (305)

Tolkien here may be alluding to the idea of Divine Providence, as I discuss below. For instance, in "The Quest for Erebor," a tale written in part to help bridge the gap between *The Hobbit*'s adventures and the events of *The Lord of the Rings*, Gandalf pointedly refers to the beneficial and lucky results that stemmed from what he called "[a] chance-meeting, as we say in Middle-earth," which seems to be intended as ironic (*Unfinished Tales* 340). But the related ideas of fate, necessity, predetermination, and so on are themselves, in some senses, figures for the vast, complex, and interconnected ensembles of narratives that constitute History. Bilbo, here as elsewhere, is reminded that he is both an agent in and subject to such dynamic historical movements.

The Lord of the Rings contains a striking scene in which Sam Gamgee has a similar, if more sudden, realization. While recalling the (to him) legendary tale of Beren and Lúthien—alluded to in the text, but not fully known to readers until *The Silmarillion* and other posthumously published writings appeared—Sam astonishes himself as he realizes that their tale, which "goes on past the happiness and into grief and beyond it" (*Two Towers* 363), continues still, several thousands of years later, and indeed that he and Frodo are part of that *same* story! In a January 30, 1945, letter to Christopher, with whom he had been sharing his drafts, Tolkien refers to this as "Sam's disquisition on the seamless web of story" (*Letters* 110). The mixed metaphor is striking. Where these stories might have been thought of as patchwork comprising discrete or even independent elements to be stitched together into a larger narrative, the "seamless" web discloses that the "great tales" never end. But the metaphor of the *web* is even more telling, since we are clearly not dealing with a more simple, linear, or teleological narrative proceeding from some distinctive *alpha* to a predetermined *omega*. Rather, we are caught up in the sticky and diverse strands of narrative, some forming more or less dense sections, others long and sinewy, with some strands seeming to lead nowhere or others apparently more important, while these values have to be reassessed as the story continues, and so on and on. The "accident" by which Bilbo discovers the One Ring in the tunnels beneath the Misty Mountains is the link that will eventually make Frodo and Sam the heroes of the most recent events in the story of Beren and Lúthian, which itself was already the long tale going back to the crafting of the jewels by Fëanor, the Flight of the Noldor from Valinor, and so forth, as readers may learn in *The Silmarillion*. But such accidents are themselves very much part of history, and what is called *chance* may also be understood as *necessity*, *fate*, or even just as *history* itself, here understood as *grand récit*. As Gandalf insists, "even the very wise cannot see all ends" (*Fellowship* 65).

Bilbo's role in *The Hobbit* provides a nice example of the way in which this philosophy of history is conceived in Tolkien, for "quite a little fellow in a wide world" is an apt description of any individual whose lifespan is measured against the tides of history. Bilbo is an unlikely hero of an epic quest, and his situation also fits well with the idea that the protagonist of the historical novel who, in Lukács's analysis, cannot be the "world-historical individual," such as Thorin Oakenshield or Bard the Dragon-Slayer, for instance, but rather a "mediocre, prosaic hero" (*Historical Novel* 34). At the beginning of *The Hobbit*, Bilbo knows little of the "wide world," and he was for the most part pleased to remain, or at least to imagine that he was, at a safe remove from it. What we witness in Bilbo's adventure is not only the expansion of the self-satisfied hobbit's geographical experience of his world—that is, by leaving the Shire and seeing new, exotic parts of Middle-earth—but also the awakening of a kind of historical consciousness, as Bilbo becomes aware of his situatedness in world history and makes his own contributions to that history. Into the mythic and epic world in which ancient elves fought in the Goblin Wars and dragons terrorized the land, Bilbo the bourgeois reluctantly ventures, and his presence signals the movement from the mythical to the historical register in the characterization of Middle-earth's world.

This vision of history as "the seamless web of story" also comports well with Tolkien's sense of the need for telling these stories. Creative writers or poets—indeed, we might call them *mythmakers*, knowing that *mythos* in Greek can also mean *account, plot,* or *story*—give form to the world by representing it and by allowing readers to experience a version of it. This is also associated with what Jameson has referred to as the "desire called Marx," which is really nothing other than the desire for narrative.

In a rare moment of autobiographical reflection, Jameson mentions that his attraction to a Marxian worldview stemmed, in part, from Sartrean existentialism, which contrary to stereotypes, "did not have the subjectivizing or psychologizing consequences often attributed to it. On the contrary," he says, "it has always seemed to me that an intense awareness of one's individual existence serves to provoke and to exacerbate an equally strong and painful sense of what transcends it, in particular of what we call History" ("Introduction," *Ideologies of Theory* xxxviii). As Jameson explains more fully,

> The time of individual human biology is radically incommensurable with the time of nature or the time of social history (or indeed, in capitalism, the time of the great economic cycles); nor is this some easily adjustable matter of *durées*, but rather a vision of interlocking, yet somehow also alternate, worlds, in which beings of brief life spans are also components of enormous and properly unimaginable totalities which develop

according to vast and inhuman rhythms, and in a different temporality altogether. The units of individual life, whatever meaning we try to give them, are never the same as those of history, even when in rare and punctual convulsions—what we call revolutions—they briefly coincide. The "desire called Marx," then, is not the will to reduce one of these dimensions to the other (in any case an impossible matter), but rather the effort to develop organs of perception capable of enabling us fitfully to position ourselves in that other temporality, that other story, over which we also hope—but now as groups and collectives, rather than as individuals—to assert some influence and control. The "desire for Marx" can therefore also be called the desire for *narrative*, if by this we understand, not some vacuous notion of "linearity" or even *telos*, but rather the impossible attempt to give representation to the multiple and incommensurable temporalities in which each of us exists. (xxxviii)

In Tolkien's larger literary and philosophical project, especially visible in *The Lord of the Rings*, which has the deep historical as well as mythic underpinnings of the "Silmarillion" materials to give it color and texture, these multiple temporalities are given form in the interlacing narrative threads. But even in the much simpler narrative of *The Hobbit*, Bilbo's awakening historical consciousness over the course of his adventures offers a vivid example.

It ought to go without saying that Tolkien's is not a Marxist philosophy of history. Given his devout religious beliefs, his idea of the movement of historical development, the fatal necessity behind the appearance of mere chance, is what we would associate with Divine Providence, whereas Marx insisted that the motor of history involved human agency, namely class struggle, even as its larger epochal movements—in particular, transitions between modes of production—could be apprehended according to "objective" or impersonal laws. But Divine Providence, like fate, is itself arguably another way of understanding history writ large, and as such religious belief is grounded in an ideology which is not altogether inconsistent with Marxist theory. Religion becomes an allegorical form, a sort of "cognitive mapping" (to cite another of Jameson's well-known ideas) by which people make sense of the larger world system that exceeds any individual's direct perception or awareness, even as the individual subject is always part of it. Indeed, as Jameson has observed, the comparison of

Marxism with religion, far from discrediting the one with the other, "may function to rewrite certain religious concepts—most notably Christian historicism and the 'concept' of providence, but also the pretheological systems of primitive magic—as anticipatory foreshadowings of historical materialism within precapitalist social formations" (*Political Unconscious* 285). If, for faithful believers like Tolkien, the ineffable will of the Almighty, moving in mysterious ways, accounts for the great trajectories of time, that can still stand as but another figure for what those operating in a Hegelian or Marxist tradition might understand as the movement of history itself.

Bringing It All Back Home

On the return journey, just as he is approaching the borders of his native land, Bilbo says to Gandalf, "our back is to legend and we are coming home," to which with wizard responds, with his customary blend of the cryptic and the matter-of-fact, "There is a long road yet" (301). The return home marks an occasion for storytelling, and it cannot be accidental that Tolkien features a final scene in which Bilbo is writing his memoirs. Having one's back to legend might seem like a way of "putting history behind us," thus being able to pause and reflect on it, but as Gandalf suggests, the road home is long, and Bilbo himself shortly thereafter recites in his poem, "Roads go ever ever on" (302).

The "desire called Marx" is really the desire for narrative. Jameson's comment resonates well with Tolkien's project, as Tolkien attempts to register these multiple temporalities that give shape both to our own personal experience and to our broader sense of history. Bilbo is fifty years old when we meet him, whereas Thorin is 195 and can personally remember the onslaught of the Lonely Mountain by Smaug some 170 years before the present; Elrond is many thousands of years old, having participated in the very Goblin Wars (i.e., the fall of Gondolin) referenced in the text, while Gandalf, though embodied in the form of a wizard, is a "maia" or angelic being who existed at the very beginning of time itself. An advantage of myth and fantasy, but also with other genres or discourses that Tolkien here exploits, is the ability to personify these disparate historical perspectives. With immortal or near-immortal characters, the visible traces of history as memory can be brought to light more easily, although one could argue that "lore" itself serves a similar purpose, hence the importance of Elrond, the one character featured in *The Hobbit*, *The Lord of the Rings*, and *The Silmarillion*, who "symbolizes throughout the ancient wisdom, and his House represents lore" (*Letters* 153).

The adventurer's return home not only brings an end to that particular story, but it makes possible the storytelling that will give these experiences their meaning. A lesson of Marx, among many others, is that those who make history are not always able to recognize that history, and there's a sense that only afterward, in bringing it all back home, can the story be told. Margaret Atwood gets at this concept in a nicely poetic way, for she notes that,

> When you are in the middle of a story it isn't a story at all, but only a confusion; a dark roaring, a blindness, a wreckage of shattered glass and splintered wood; like a house in a whirlwind, or else a boat crushed by the icebergs or swept over the rapids, and all aboard powerless to stop it. It's only afterwards that it becomes anything like a story at all. When you are telling it, to yourself or to someone else. (*Alias Grace* 298)

That Tolkien chooses to end *The Hobbit* with a scene in which Bilbo is writing his memoirs, thus self-consciously attempting to make sense of his experiences and to give form to his impressions, cannot be accidental. Bilbo's proposed titled, "There and Back Again, a Hobbit's Holiday," is not accidental either, since being "back again" makes possible his historiography. Perhaps it is not surprising that the final line of *The Lord of the Rings*, uttered by Samwise Gamgee—who, as we know, will eventually take up the pen and contribute his own chapters to the Red Book of Westmarch, thus adding his part to Bilbo's tale, which is to say, to history itself—is "Well, I'm back" (*Return* 340).

The homecoming of Bilbo Baggins marks the end of his adventure, but it establishes him and his home *in* that larger historical and geographical system which he had been content previously to ignore. The great narrative of history, like roads going ever ever on, will be filled with nasty, disturbing, uncomfortable things, but the adventure proves to be well worth it.

4

Show Me Now Your Map: Toward a Literary Cartography of Middle-earth

After the title page, the first element of the story the reader of *The Hobbit* is likely to encounter is an image of Thrór's Map. Of course, this is not surprising; maps have been part of books for as long as there have been books. No matter how vividly places and spaces are depicted within the language of the text, writers and readers have frequently also desired figural or pictographic representations of those places and spaces, and it is certainly not uncommon to pause in one's reading to consult the map at various stages in one's experience of the narrative, much as would travelers themselves in strange territories pull out their maps from time to time. With imaginary places, such as fantastic, science fictional, or utopian realms—the original 1516 publication of *Utopia* by Thomas More featured a map of the island nation, for instance—the desire for an actual map may be stronger still, as readers presumably cannot rely on any store of "real world" geographical knowledge they might bring to the text in advance.

The map appearing at the beginning of *The Hobbit* is thus a relatively conventional element, at least at first glance. Even before Tolkien, but certainly after the success of *The Hobbit* and *The Lord of the Rings*,

© The Author(s), under exclusive license to Springer Nature Switzerland AG 2022
R. T. Tally Jr., *J. R. R. Tolkien's* The Hobbit,
Palgrave Science Fiction and Fantasy: A New Canon,
https://doi.org/10.1007/978-3-031-11266-9_4

novels in the fantasy genre are almost expected to include maps. Maps are arguably such a staple of the fantasy genre in general that to not include a map would seem eccentric. Indeed, in *The Color of Magic* (1983), the first volume in the vast Discworld series that simultaneously embodies and spoofs fantasy conventions, Terry Pratchett felt the need to include this caveat in his Foreword, published six years after the novel first appeared:

> There are no maps. You can't map a sense of humor. Anyway, what is a fantasy map but a space beyond which There Be Dragons? On the Discworld we know that There Be Dragons Everywhere. They might not all have scales and forked tongues, but they Be Here all right, grinning and jostling and trying to sell you souvenirs. (n.p.)

In contrast to Tolkien, who so meticulously attempted to integrate and make consistent the elements of his *legendarium* (especially in later life), Pratchett gleefully admits on the same page that "[t]he Discworld is not a coherent fantasy world. Its geography is fuzzy, its chronology unreliable." This is not only true of Pratchett's fictional world, but part of the fun of it. Still, the fact that he felt the need to inform readers in advance is itself evidence of the cartographic conventions of the genre.

In *The Hobbit*, there are two maps: Thrór's Map and the Wilderland Map. In this chapter I will discuss both in the context of a broader *literary cartography* developed across the course of the novel. (By "literary cartography," I mean the figurative representation of the spaces of the world in the writing itself, distinct from though perhaps related to, the images on any graphic maps that might also be provided.) Thrór's Map, which serves multiple purposes in and around the text, operates as a diagram and as a plot element, and thus doubly contributes to the shaping of Middle-earth's geography in the narrative. Unlike the Wilderland Map, which like most maps appearing in novels seems to be a largely paratextual element included for the benefit of the reader (in this case, helping the reader to visualize the spaces traversed by Bilbo Baggins and other characters in the story), Thrór's Map is a crucial item *within* the story. Without the map, the story cannot happen, at least not in the way that it does, and the rediscovery of the lost map by Gandalf is itself a key moment in the history of Thorin's quest to reclaim the Kingdom under the Mountain. In Rivendell, Elrond says to Thorin, "show me now your map!" and while examining it discovers the "moon-letters," hidden writing made visible only by the light of the appropriate moon, which illuminate and supplement the geographical knowledge figured forth in the map with narrative information necessary for using the key, for the secret message explains how to locate the hidden doorway (52–53). As with these artifacts, the map and the key, the literary cartography of Tolkien's world will involve a dynamic interplay of descriptive and narrative processes.

Thrór's Map: The Hidden Entrance to Middle-earth

Within the novel, Thrór's Map is unveiled by Gandalf during the "unexpected party" in the first chapter. Dinner having been finished and dishes cleaned and put away, the wizard, dwarves, and hobbit settle down to discuss the business at hand. Thorin reveals the Quest for Erebor (as Tolkien would call it in a 1954 narrative included in *Unfinished Tales*), that is, the plan to retake his ancestral kingdom at the Lonely Mountain far to the east from the dragon Smaug who had forced Thorin and his people into exile. As the dwarves debate how they might enter the mountain, at the same time wondering whether Bilbo will be of much use to them, Gandalf spreads out the map on the table. At first, Thorin dismisses it entirely, saying "I don't see that this will help us much [...] I remember the Mountain well enough and the lands about it" (20). But Gandalf then adverts their attention, not to geographic figures on the map, but to the drawing of a hand with its index finger extended, pointing in the direction of the Lonely Mountain, and to a message written in runes: "that is the secret entrance. You see that rune on the West side, and the hand pointing to it from the other runes? That marks a hidden passage to the Lower Halls" (20). A somewhat awkward, parenthetical interpolation by the narrator lets the reader know to "look at the map at the beginning of this book." Hence, both for the reader and for Thorin and Company, the map is an integral part of the story.

As Gandalf observes, the map's most important feature at this point lies in its revelation of a hidden entrance to the Lonely Mountain, one that the dragon might be unaware of and, in any case, one that is too small for the dragon to use. Acknowledging that the secret entrance is likely invisible as well, that is, "made to look exactly like the side of the mountain," Gandalf adds, "I forgot to mention that with the map went a key, a small and curious key. Here it is!" and hands it to Thorin. It will not be until the party reaches Rivendell in Chapter III, when Elrond discovers and translates the "moon-letters" on Thrór's Map, that the full import of the key will be realized, but for the moment, as Thorin puts it, "things begin to look more hopeful" (21). The plan will be to infiltrate the mountain through this hidden doorway, and that is indeed how Bilbo and the dwarves find their way inside, but a great deal of history and geography stands in the way first.

Some of that history is touched on in the conversation that follows. Thorin tells Bilbo of the Kingdom under the Mountain established by his grandfather Thrór, of the nearby prosperous town of Dale with its own human king, and of the sacking and destruction of both by the dragon Smaug. Thorin himself was spared death by the good fortune of having been outside at the time, and only later was he joined by his father and grandfather who had mysteriously escaped. The revelation of the secret passage only minutes earlier was the first time Thorin realized that this must have been their salvation. This leads him to ask how Gandalf had "got hold of" the map, which obviously should have come to him by birthright, and Gandalf reveals the rest of his story. After the fall of the Lonely Mountain to Smaug, Thorin's grandfather was killed in the mines of Moria by Azog the goblin, and Thorin's father Thráin kept the map and key. But before Thráin could return to the north to try to use them, he was captured by the Necromancer (i.e., Sauron), and driven to madness, "witless and wandering," in his dungeons. Gandalf discovered him—"and a nasty dangerous business it was. Even I, Gandalf, only just escaped" (26)—and was given the map and key, but Thráin did not even know his own name at that stage, and it took Gandalf some time to find Thorin and, at last, turn these heirlooms over to him.

The backstory of finding the map and key is noteworthy, as it helps to tie the narrative of *The Hobbit* to the larger *legendarium*, which will also be fundamental to the continuity of the tales taken up in *The Lord of the Rings*. The reference to the Necromancer is particularly important, even though he plays no further visible role in *The Hobbit*. (Tolkien's subsequent writings would reveal that, while Bilbo and the dwarves were contending spiders and elves in Mirkwood, Gandalf and the other members of the White Council were battling Sauron, also known as the Necromancer, in Dol Guldur, a fortress in southern Mirkwood.) This is somewhat relevant to the plot of *The Hobbit*, insofar as Thorin feels that he and the dwarves ought to avenge themselves on the Necromancer once they have settled their scores with Smaug. Gandalf, tellingly, rebukes him: "Don't be absurd! He is an enemy far beyond the powers of all the dwarves put together, if they could all be collected from the four corners of the world" (26). This terrible presence owes something to Tolkien's personal passion for the "Silmarillion" materials, which he could not quite abandon even when writing a different sort of work for children. As he put it,

> the construction of elaborate and consistent mythology (and two languages) rather occupies the mind, and the Silmarils are in my heart. [...] Mr. Baggins began as a comic tale among conventional and inconsistent Grimm's fairy-tale dwarves, and got drawn into the edge of it—so that even Sauron the terrible peeped over the edge. (*Letters* 26)

But Sauron's appearance also goes to the heart of Tolkien's sense of how fairy stories, that is, tales that take place in "Faërie" or "the perilous realm," ought to operate. In another letter, responding in particular to the idea that the Necromancer's story would be "too dark" for some readers, Tolkien avers, "actually the presence (even if only on the borders) of the terrible is, I believe, what gives this imagined world its verisimilitude. A safe fairyland is untrue to all worlds" (*Letters* 24). The Middle-earth as we come to know it in *The Hobbit* is thus made "true," as is our own world, in part because of this encounter with "the terrible," which is figured here as the vaster historical and geographical world system in which this adventure takes place.

As artifacts, then, Thrór's Map and the key that comes with it are bound up in this larger history, and the map itself functions as a sort of hidden entrance to the larger world of Middle-earth. In addition, the map is still helpful for readers who wish to get a sense of the places it depicts, the Lonely Mountain and its environs. Interestingly enough, in what might be an almost *realistic* touch, Tolkien has oriented the map in such a way that the East is at the top, the North at the left. This was consistent with medieval European diagrams, such as the *orbis terrarum* or T-and-O maps which faced east—the very word *orientation* literally means to face east—toward the Orient (and, in line with religious interpretations, Jerusalem represented the central point, with Asia "above," Europe and Africa in their respective zones "below"). Tolkien's mythology is definitively stated to be pre-Christian, but this distinctive orientation of the ancient map offers a bit of cartographic verisimilitude to the medieval worldview of the Holy Roman Empire, thus implicitly relating the imaginary world to European history. By being *of* the world, Thrór's Map offers readers an entrée into both its spaces and its history. Thus, the map makes possible the adventure in which the literary cartography of Middle-earth is rendered knowable.

The Edge of the Wild

Speaking specifically of *The Lord of the Rings*, but it may suit *The Hobbit* as well, Tolkien declared, "I wisely started with a map, and made the story fit (generally with meticulous care for distances). The other way about lands one in confusions and impossibilities, and in any case it is weary work to compose a map from a story" (*Letters* 177). Tolkien here refers to the practical dilemma of making sure that movements across space and within time are properly registered in the story. Tom Shippey has asserted that *The Lord of the Rings* is charactered by a "cartographic plot" (*Road* 94–134), an observation that might also apply to *The Hobbit*, but in a much more limited way. Obviously, in *The Lord of the Rings*, which covers far more territory in far more complex ways than its predecessor, the potential for confusion is amplified. Also, in that novel, many "journeys" are taking place simultaneously, as in some cases three or four different sets of protagonists must be tracked at various places on the map at roughly the same time. (For instance, after the breaking of the Fellowship at the conclusion of Book II, Frodo and Sam, Merry and Pippen, and Aragorn, Gimli, and Legolas form three distinct parties respectively, with adventures taking place in different regions; the entire ensemble, including Gandalf who was "sent back" after his fatal battle with the Balrog, but minus Boromir, who perished in the opening chapter on Book III, are reunited in Gondor only near the end, after the ring's destruction.) In *The Hobbit*, both the narrative and the geography are far simpler, as the story is focalized on a single main character, Bilbo, in almost every chapter—in "Fire and Water," the narrative cuts away to Esgaroth (Lake-town) to follow the exploits of Smaug, Bard, and the people of that town, for instance—and the entire adventure takes place only a relatively narrow section of the northern part of Tolkien's imaginary world. But even so, the world system that becomes visible in *The Hobbit* is culturally diverse and topographically heterogeneous, while also forming an integrated whole.

Just as "the seamless web of story" illuminates the historical intercon-nectedness of seemingly discrete and separate events, Tolkien's geograph-ical consciousness requires that the various lands, which may appear to be distinct and largely cut off in various ways from one another, be viewed as part of a larger, integrated world system. Bilbo's *adventures* disclose the reality of a broader "grand narrative" of history through the unassuming anti-heroics of an anachronistic fish-out-of-water, and Bilbo's encoun-ters with the different landscapes, enclaves, races, and cultures during his long eastward journey to the Lonely Mountain (and, to a much lesser extent perhaps, on his return journey home) make this world "real" both for him, of course, but also for a reader who, in seeing the connections between different imaginary spaces in Tolkien's otherworld, begins to descry the often unseen but essential lines connecting disparate places in our own world.

In a telling moment in *The Lord of the Rings*, Frodo cites Bilbo, who "used often to say there was only one Road; that is was like a great river: its springs were at every doorstep, and every path was its tribu-tary" (*Fellowship* 82). He then quotes Bilbo directly, referring to "the path outside the front door at Bag End": "Do you realize that this is the very path that goes through Mirkwood, and that if you let it, it might take you to the Lonely Mountain or even further and to worse places?" (82).

And it is true! Although the Wilderland Map in *The Hobbit* does not show the full extent of the area, the "Old Forest Road" it depicts is the same East Road that leads out of Hobbiton. Had Thorin and Company not been waylaid by goblins and beset with other problems along the way, they might well have been able to march down a relatively well-established avenue all the way to the river south of Lake-town, which seems to have been the initial plan, according to Thorin (*Hobbit* 21). At the beginning of *The Hobbit*, the extent of Bilbo's geographical knowledge was mostly limited to a small portion of The Shire, but even so, "He loved maps, and in his hall there hung a large one of the Country Round with all his favorite walks marked on it in red ink" (21). Marking his favorite walks on a map shows the way that he sees the itinerary and the map together at once, of course. His somewhat zig-zagging eastward itinerary in the course of his adventures, combined with a more speculative sense of the abstract spaces traversed, would give Bilbo a clearer idea of the geographic totality.

The literary cartography of Middle-earth emerges in *The Hobbit* through the dialectical interplay of the itinerary and the map. This distinction has been made by various scholars in different contexts, but I am especially interested in the way that it plays out in the form of the narrative. Michel de Certeau, for instance, in his discussion of "spatial stories" distinguishes between the itinerary (or tour) and the map, but he strongly favors the former; he views itinerary as a discursive practice in which the mobile subject opens up potentially new spaces, "writing the city" while moving about it, whereas the map is characterized as imposing a static, hegemonic totalization from above (Certeau 119). But as Kevin Lynch's iconic study *The Image of the City* makes clear, the successful navigation of a given space by "wayfinding" individuals depends very much on the "imageability" of the city itself, which is to say, on how capable the pedestrians are at forming their own mental maps. The inability to map is profoundly alienating. (In *The Lord of the Rings*, a disoriented Pippin "wished now that he had learned more in Rivendell, and looked more at maps and things" [*Two Towers* 52].) As Fredric Jameson has observed in his discussion of cognitive mapping, which draws upon Lynch's model, itineraries are basically "diagrams organized around the still subject-centered or existential journey of the traveler," whereas *mapping* proper will require "the coordination of existential data (the empirical position of the subject) with unlived, abstract conceptions of the geographic totality" (*Postmodernism* 51–52). For individual or collective subjects moving through and about a given space, the tracing of subjective itineraries and the projection of a supra-subjective map are likely both required at all times, and the coordination among these two registers is part of the broader cartographic imperative that informs our engagement with social spaces in general.

In *The Hobbit*, the apprehension of a sort of geographic totality does not merely come from the graphic maps printed at the beginning of the book, though they can contribute to it in their limited way. Rather, it develops across the novel's pages through the adventures of the characters, and Bilbo's own dawning sense of the geographic, and the geopolitical, framework of his world mirrors that of the reader, who gains knowledge of the world through various episodes and the connections between them. The narrative elements, including the relating of Bilbo's experiences in these places, yield greater knowledge and understanding of this geography than the figured surface of the map alone could provide, although that is obviously useful as well, and the sections in which the narrator pauses to describe the scene or events help to flesh out the details of those places. In this sense, literary cartography, much like Jameson's notion of cognitive mapping, is not a strictly spatial endeavor, but is intimately associated with the problems of narrative itself. How we *know* the world is largely a function of our ability to tell stories about it, to bring it into cognizable form in the shape of a story or a number of stories. The literary map of Middle-earth that emerges in *The Hobbit* is not simply to be gleaned from the graphics featured on Thrór's Map or the Wilderland Map, but comes into being through the subjective experiences of Bilbo and others in the text, alongside the more objective realities, the structural or systemic forms in which such experiences are made possible and take on meaning.

When Bilbo, Thorin, and the other dwarves are about to enter Mirkwood, Gandalf takes leave of them, not before noting that "There are no safe paths in this part of the world. Remember you are over the Edge of the Wild now, and in for all sorts of fun wherever you go" (138). That designation, "the Edge of the Wild," appears a number of times in

The Hobbit, always with reference to peril, but it seems awfully vague. However, the Wilderland Map features the actual line that demarcates the "edge" in question, and consulting the map, we see that the company passed over the "edge of the wild" before their encounter with the trolls in Chapter II. Indeed, we realize that all these adventures take place "over the Edge of the Wild on the borders of the unknown" (99). The knowledge of such places does not necessarily make them less dangerous, but it does make them more meaningful, as they become integral to Bilbo's world and to our own.

Roads Go Ever Ever On

The Hobbit is a tale of a journey, and it is thus quite apt that Bilbo—the putative author of the tale, even if that conceit does not quite square with the narrative voice, its tone, and its frequent asides—bestowed upon it the title "There and Back Again." For most of the novel, the narrative proceeds in accordance with the new places that the protagonist visits. The episodic nature of the story, in which each chapter more or less embodies a kind of mini-adventure from which the larger adventure constructs itself, allows us to see each place in its own, almost unique frame, but in the aggregate, an entire world system becomes visible. In this way, *The Hobbit* almost enacts a kind of montage, whereby a series of more limited images forms a whole that surpasses the mere sum of the parts.

As Shippey has noted, for all the geographic novelty of Tolkien's world, in *The Hobbit* there are almost no toponyms that are not simply descriptive (see *Road* 96). In contrast to the linguistic abundance of *The Lord of the Rings*, in which a given place may have multiple names (i.e., those given by elves, men, dwarves, or orcs, say), in *The Hobbit* most places are labeled as they appear from the perspective of the onlooker: Hobbiton is a town of hobbits; Rivendell is in a dell carved out (or "riven") by a river; the Misty Mountains are mist-enveloped; Mirkwood is murky (although is was, and would again become, known as Greenwood); Lake-town is a town on a lake; and the Lonely Mountain is a singular prominent mountain towering above the adjacent hills. An amusing exception, perhaps, may be found when Bilbo asks why a certain somebody (Beorn) calls a place "the Carrock," to which Gandalf responds, "He called it the Carrock, because carrock is his word for it. He calls things like that carrocks, and this one is *the* Carrock because it is the only one near his home and he knows it well" (115). (Intriguingly, this odd name too might be mostly descriptive, as it seems to combine the Celtic *carr*, referring to isolated rocks protruding from the water, with the English *rock* [see Rateliff, *History* 261–266].) There are a few elvish place names in the text, like Moria or Esgaroth, but these are quite rare overall. Of course, even "proper" names are often etymologically derived from descriptive terms, only that we've forgotten those meanings. As Shippey says, names "are arbitrary, even if they were not so in the beginning. [...] In the modern world we take them as labels, as things accordingly in a very close one-to-one relationship with whatever they label" (*Road* 101). In *The Hobbit*, the fact that these "names" are given as descriptive of their respective places indicates the degree to which the perceiver, the individual or collective subject who looks upon such places, *defines* them. The overlapping of the itinerary and the map is evident here as well, since the wandering "subject" looking upon the mountains, say, would recognize their mistiness, and the "objective" name would be set on the map thereafter.

As we have seen, *The Hobbit*'s narrative is quite episodic, and until Bilbo confronts Smaug in Chapter XII each chapter features a new place, and most of the chapters involve an encounter with a new race or culture as well. Beginning in the first chapter, where the reader meets Bilbo, Gandalf, and the dwarves, the following chapters introduce a wild place with trolls, Rivendell and elves, Goblin-town and goblins, Gollum's cave, the wargs' gathering spot, the eagles' eyrie, the Carrock and Beorn, Mirkwood and spiders, the kingdom of the wood-elves, Lake-town and men, and eventually the Lonely Mountain and its dragon. In the next chapter I will discuss the racial and cultural aspects of this territorial division, for it is remarkable that Tolkien depicts each recognizable place in Middle-earth as almost entirely racially homogeneous. But it is also worth noting that this set-up allows Bilbo to encounter its place and each culture in an episodic fashion, thus helping to establish a serialized and cumulative sense of the world system, while still engaged in a seemingly personal adventure. The narrative form determines the geographical and geopolitical framework in which the events of the plot take place.

The episodic structure of the narrative in *The Hobbit* also affects the sense of geographical distance, as vast swaths of land can be covered in an instant, in order for the onrushing plot to arrive at the next episode. For example, in Chapter II, Bilbo hastily joins the Dwarves at The Green Dragon Inn, which is just over a mile from his home at Bag-End. The next adventure will concern the trolls, who occupy the Trollshaws (not named as such in *The Hobbit*) near the foot of the Misty Mountains, nearly 400 miles or so away (e.g., it is 412 to Rivendell [see Rateliff, *History* 815, 826]). According to John D. Rateliff, this journey took the company 27 days, but the entirety of these travels is covered in a single paragraph of *The Hobbit*:

> At first they had passed through hobbit-lands, a wide respectable country inhabited by decent folk, with good roads, an inn or two, and now and then a dwarf or a farmer ambling by on business. Then they came to lands where people spoke strangely, and sang songs Bilbo had never heard before. Now they had gone on far into the Lone-lands, where there were no people left, no inns, and the roads grew steadily worse. Not far ahead were dreary hills, rising higher and higher, dark with trees. On some of them were old castles with an evil look, as if they had been built by wicked people. Everything seemed gloomy, for the weather that day had taken a nasty turn. Mostly it had been as good as May can be, even in merry tales, but now it was cold and wet. In the Lone-lands they had been obliged to camp when they could, but at least it had been dry. (31)

By way of comparison, if not an entirely fair one, we might note that Frodo's party comes across these same trolls some 232 pages into *The Lord of the Rings* (or some 150 pages after Frodo leaves Hobbiton). Of course, Frodo's trajectory is less direct, carrying him far off the East Road at times, but even so he will experience in some detail both the distances and the places mentioned in this brief paragraph from *The Hobbit*. For this paragraph already indicates, to knowing readers of the sequel, the town of Bree ("where people spoke strangely"), the apparently unpopulated lands near the Midgewater Marshes, the Weather Hills, and perhaps

Weathertop itself ("old castles with an evil look"). But in Bilbo's tale, no adventures worth mentioning are to be had in these places.

In Rivendell, the narrator explains another feature of this episodic story: "Now it is a strange thing, but things that are good to have and days that are good to spend are soon told about, and not much to listen to; while things that are uncomfortable, palpitating, and even gruesome, may make a good tale, and take a deal of telling anyway." Thus, while Bilbo, Gandalf, and the dwarves spend at least two weeks in Rivendell, "there is little to tell about their stay" (51). Rivendell, the site of the Last Homely House west of the mountains, is a place in which adventures do not happen, for as Tolkien once remarked, "Elrond symbolizes throughout the ancient wisdom, and his House represents Lore [...] It is not a scene of *action* but of *reflection*. This is a place visited on the way to all deeds, or 'adventures'" (*Letters* 153). Hence it makes sense that Rivendell, an "enchanted sanctuary," is where the company rests, rehabilitates, and also gains valuable knowledge. Elrond's discovery and translation of the moon letters on Thrór's Map turns out to be essential to the success of Thorin's mission, after all, and Elrond also provides a tantalizing glimpse into the vast historical record when he identifies Thorin's and Gandalf's swords as having been forged in Gondolin during "the Goblin-wars," another brief vista into the "Silmarillion" materials, as the Fall of Gondolin took place thousands of years earlier. Each "pause" in the overall adventure tale of *The Hobbit* helps to shape the historical and geographical reality of Middle-earth.

After the adventures have concluded and Bilbo returns to his native land, he recites the poem beginning "*Roads go ever ever on*," which ends with the stanza:

> *Eyes that fire and sword have seen*
> > *And horror in the halls of stone*
> *Look at last on meadows green*
> > *And trees and hills they long have known.* (302, italics in original)

As Gandalf notes, "You are not the hobbit that you were," and Bilbo's poem reflects the *sense* of the adventure, insofar is its meaning "comes home" to him as he himself returns to his actual home. The "roads" are never-ending, of course, but one can only go so far on them. For Bilbo—and, in a somewhat allegorical sense, for the reader as well—the journey, punctuated throughout by the enclaves visited along the way, made this larger world *real*. Not only has the map become more vivid and detailed, but the world itself, its history and its geography, have become part of Bilbo's very being. Although his own adventures have mostly come to an end, the world in which all adventures happen now takes on a substantive reality that it previously lacked.

Plus Ultra: Gandalf's Peregrinations

Bilbo's return to Bag-End not only represents a "bringing it all back home" of his adventure, but highlights the limitations of the domestic enclave itself, which is in many respects a form that, whether intended by its inhabitants or not, effectively shuts off "the world," along with its history, from one's own place. Hobbits are, after all, depicted as being rather provincial, parochial, and extremely suspicious of all things outside their purview. Tolkien's frequent references to Bilbo's "Tookish side," provides a shorthand way of indicating that adventurousness, even at the rather modest level of taking an interest in the outside world, is considered *outré* at the very least. Bilbo's subsequent worldliness, being an elf-friend and hosting dwarves, costs him his reputation and made him "queer" in the eyes of his folk, though he did not mind (303–304).

Outside of the hobbit culture, where people were more attuned with the ways of the world, perhaps it was different, but there was still presumably a sense of settled place that trumped the desire for greater cosmopolitanism (a term Tolkien found especially abhorrent, in fact). There was travel and trade, but each enclave in the world of *The Hobbit* maintains its own culture, often determined in part by racialism. The exception is literally embodied in the figure of Gandalf, the "wandering wizard" who has no particular home in the Middle-earth. In a world where most people seem to stay put within their native communities or fortified redoubts, Gandalf is notable for his peripatetic character. His movements take place beyond the edges of most characters' more familiar maps, and he is the instigator of adventures beyond one's borders, as

Bilbo marvels at the beginning of the novel: "Not the Gandalf who was responsible for so many quiet lads and lasses going off into the Blue for mad adventures? Anything from climbing trees to visiting elves—or sailing in ships, sailing to other shores?" (5–6). The wizard represents that enchanting worldliness that make "the Blue" and "other shores" part of one's own world.

Gandalf is not exactly symbolic of the world and of history, but he functions as a catalytic agent in bringing the world and history into consciousness. In *The Lord of the Rings*, readers learn that he bears the third Elven Ring, Narya, which was given to him by the great elven leader Círdan the Shipwright upon Gandalf's arrival: "For this is the Ring of Fire, and with it you may rekindle hearts in a world that grows chill" (*Return of the King*, Appendix B, 403). Within Tolkien's works, Gandalf cannot help but appear as an *agent provocateur*, a meddler in the business of others and bringer of bad news, as several of his detractors note. But in this way he also brings people together and makes visible, if not also forging, the connections among the various enclaves and peoples of Middle-earth. He is thus integral to what Tolkien refers to as the "world-politics" of Middle-earth (see *Letters* 138–139).

Starting with his appearance on Bilbo's doorstep and then at the "unexpected party" in Chapter I, Gandalf enters the scene four times in *The Hobbit*, which means he also exits thrice; where he goes each time is shrouded in some mystery, but it is always understood that he is engaged in some important matter that is ultimately to the benefit of all. In Chapter II, just before their encounter with the trolls, Thorin and the others discover that Gandalf has disappeared, but of course he returns just in time to save them. When Thorin asks why he had left them in the first place, Gandalf responds, "To look ahead"; when asked what brought him back "in the nick of time," he says "Looking back" (43). That minor scouting mission alerted him to the menace of trolls and also put him in touch with elves from Rivendell, both matters of great pragmatic value. Later he briefly disappears after killing a number of goblins in the cave in the Misty Mountains only to reappear in time to assassinate the Great Goblin and lead the dwarves to safety. Finally, and most importantly, he takes leave of the company at the edge of Mirkwood because of "some pressing business away south" (136), only to return just before the Battle of Five Armies. Tolkien in a letter referred to this as the only point where "these 'world-politics' act as part of the mechanism of the story": "Gandalf the Wizard is called away on high business, an attempt to deal with the menace of the Necromancer, and so leaves the Hobbit without help or advice in the midst of his 'adventure,' forcing him to stand on his own legs, and become in his mode heroic" (158–159). Gandalf's *absences* are thus crucial to the plot of *The Hobbit*, but also to the establishment of a larger world order beyond the mere quests of the heroes of the story.

The reference to the Necromancer recalls the early scene in which Gandalf reveals Thrór's Map and the accompanying key. Gandalf reveals that he had acquired these artifacts from Thrain, who was "a prisoner in the dungeons of the Necromancer," and Thorin asks "Whatever were you doing there?" with "a shudder." Gandalf answers, "Never you mind. I was finding things out, as usual" (26). The "as usual" is perhaps more significant than the perilous adventure that he refuses to relate. Gandalf's movements about the grander map of Middle-earth are themselves part of the overall knowledge of Middle-earth, geographical and historical, and as he's "finding things out," that world becomes richer and more nuanced. Gandalf is in this sense the *key* to the literary cartography of Middle-earth, for he makes possible the knowledge of its disparate places and spaces.

5

More Dangerous and Less Wise: Race, Class, and the Geopolitical Order

Just after the fearsome battle with the giant spiders who dwell in Mirkwood, Bilbo Baggins encounters elves for the second time in his life, but he finds them rather unlike those he had met at Elrond's Last Homely House in Rivendell. As Tolkien (or the narrator) explains, these were Wood-elves. "They differed from the High Elves of the West, and were more dangerous and less wise," but after explaining their differences from "the Light-elves and Deep-elves and Sea-elves," the narrator concludes, "Still elves they were and remain, and that is Good People" (167–168). All elves in Tolkien's world are "good people," but here readers learn of the hierarchies even among them, and from the perspective of Bilbo and the dwarves, these elves constitute an obstacle to the success of their quest nearly as great as some they had previously overcome, such as the trolls, goblins, wargs, or spiders. Whereas the elves of Rivendell had provided welcome rest, refreshment, and knowledge, the elves of Mirkwood offer Thorin and Company menace and imprisonment (though, in fairness, they are relatively well treated while in the Elvenking's cells).

By introducing a second, rather different sort of elves at this point in the tale, Tolkien further elaborates the breadth and diversity of the world

© The Author(s), under exclusive license to Springer Nature
Switzerland AG 2022
R. T. Tally Jr., *J. R. R. Tolkien's* The Hobbit,
Palgrave Science Fiction and Fantasy: A New Canon,
https://doi.org/10.1007/978-3-031-11266-9_5

system that Bilbo, and the readers, come to know throughout the course of the novel. As befits the episodic form of the narrative, perhaps, a new creature, culture, or "race" is introduced in almost every chapter of *The Hobbit*, at least until Bilbo and the dwarves arrive at the Lonely Mountain and meet the dragon. In the course of these encounters, the racial hierarchy of Tolkien's world also becomes more visible; these various races or types of people are not merely different, which is not surprising, but in a sense *ranked*. As with the Wood-elves with respect to the High Elves of the West, they are even ranked within a given "racial" category, but overall the system of racial difference in Tolkien's world becomes its own form of class system, which in turn structures the geopolitical order of Middle-earth as a whole.

With each identified race, there are subdivisions that designate some high or low, often determined by heredity or birthright, but not necessarily excluding the idea of social or economic class, which might be determined by wealth or property. (As we saw in Chapter 2, such distinctions among social classes may have more to do with manners than with money, and can be discerned through speech patterns or politeness.) Better known, though often still implicit, are the hierarchies *between* the various races, such that while descendants of the Númenoreans may be considered superior to other men in *The Lord of the Rings*, men in general (as well as dwarves, hobbits, and, of course, orcs) would still be spiritually, morally, and even politically subordinate to the elves. In *Tolkien, Race, and Cultural History*, Dimitra Fimi has analyzed the "hierarchical world" that serves as the basis for racial and cultural difference in Tolkien's work, and many other scholars have explored in detail both the racial and racist ideologies in Middle-earth and in Tolkien's own background. Although some would argue that the fantasy genre tends toward oversimplification, particularly in establishing largely homogeneous monocultures in the various enclaves, Tolkien's is a rather complex, multicultural world system on the whole.

What Is a Race?

The very idea of "race" is fraught with difficulties. For the most part, in this discussion, I am sticking with the definition of a *race* that has become rather commonplace in the discourse around fantasy as a genre. Terry Pratchett has half-jokingly referred to such conventions with reference to the "consensus fantasy universe" in which "elves are tall and fair and use bows, dwarves are small and dark and vote Labour" ("Why Gandalf Never Married"). Hence, in this schema, the different *orders* of sentient beings constitute races, as opposed to, for instance, the idea of skin color or other phenotypical differences being used to characterize racial difference within a given species. Yet it is clear even then that those other kinds of racial markers play their role in Tolkien and in fantasy literature more broadly, and one cannot help but notice the ways that physical characteristics, such as "fair" *versus* "swarthy," are almost always regarded as having moral significance. Moreover, the cultural differences both among and within various "races" are themselves often signaled in Tolkien through a related genetic or hereditary condition, such that higher orders of men, for instance, can lose their nobility by breeding with "lesser" men.

As Raymond Williams points out in *Keywords*, the English word *race*, "of uncertain origin […] had been used in the sense of a common stock" since the sixteenth century (213); tellingly, Williams mentions this in his entry for "Nationalist," for he does not even include "Race" as one of his keywords in the original book. (In the 1983 expanded edition of *Keywords*, "Racial," which only comes into English in the nineteenth-century and has a profound effect on racialist and racist attitudes in the era in which Tolkien was born and raised, is included.) The confusing ways in which the word race has been understood over the years has, unsurprisingly, had significant effects across cultures and societies. As Williams goes on to say,

> Physical, cultural and socio-economic differences are taken up, projected and generalized, and so confused that different kinds of variation are made to stand for or imply each other. The prejudice and cruelty that then often follow, or that are rationalized by the confusions, are not only

evil in themselves; they have also profoundly complicated, and in certain areas placed under threat, the necessary language of the (non-prejudicial) recognition of human diversity and its actual communities. (250)

Needless to say, maybe, but the term and its definition continues to bear complex ideological and conceptual difficulties. Moreover, no amount of data, argument, or knowledge proving that race is a fundamentally unscientific, artificial, and all too often mendaciously biased construct can counter the simple fact that race, along with racism, remains socially significant and very much real. Not surprisingly, Tolkien Studies is one of many areas in which much needed, if also heated, debates about the role of race are taking place in the twenty-first century. Robert Stuart's *Tolkien, Race, and Racism in Middle-earth* provides an impressive survey of the topic, from Tolkien's own time up to the present, and it makes a convincing case for recognizing the racialism and racism in Tolkien's work and in his own personal views, in part as a necessary counter to the many white supremacists who wish to claim Tolkien for themselves.

In *The Hobbit*, this hierarchical system of race is visible, but it is not as pronounced and much more simple than in *The Lord of the Rings*. *The Hobbit*'s races are, for the most part, separate (if not equal), and each is located in its own distinctive enclave. For instance, aside from a few scattered references to others made in passing, there are the elves of Rivendell and of Mirkwood, men of Lake-town (and Dale), dwarves of the Iron Hills, plus those of Thorin's company and references to Moria, and goblins of the Misty Mountain and of Gundabad in the North, as well as the distinctive characters who live apart from others, like Gollum or Beorn. Thus, in *The Hobbit* the political geography of Middle-earth is also rather racialized, as the places on the map are associated not only with their respective inhabitants, but with those inhabitants' racial character.

As such, the races frequently substitute for whole cultures, nations, and classes as well, although as we see with the Wood-elves, there are meaningful subdivisions. For Bilbo, who prior to this adventure had presumably had little experience with people who were not fellow hobbits, each new "race" seems to represent an almost homogeneous culture; that is, in each case, he is introduced not only to the persons he encounters directly, but to that entire "type" of being. The Battle of Five Armies, arguably the climactic event of *The Hobbit*, is named as much for the races involved as for the "armies" per se. For example, Dain's army is made up of forces distinct from Thorin's, who have come from a different part of the map altogether, and yet presumably all dwarves are counted as a single army among the five. Here *race* is quite broadly conceived, since one of those races is apparently "Wild Wolves": "it was called the Battle of Five Armies, and it was terrible. Upon one side were the Goblins and the Wild Wolves, and upon the other were Elves and Men and Dwarves" (281). The name of the battle notwithstanding, the tide turns when another "army," made up of the eagles, arrives and helps to eliminate the goblins' advantage in the mountains. Even so, it is not until Beorn appears as a sort of "army of one"—"He came alone, and in bear's shape; and he seemed to have grown almost to giant-size in his wrath" (291)—and slays the goblin leader Bolg and his bodyguard, that the day is won. Bilbo is himself a combatant, but mostly stays out of the fray before getting knocked unconscious and thus missing the conclusion of the battle. "It was the most dreadful of all Bilbo's experiences, and the one which at the time he hated most—which is to say it was the one he was most proud of, and most fond of recalling long afterwards, although he was quite unimportant in it" (283). To the extent that Bilbo himself joined an "army," he chose to side with the elves.

In Tolkien's *legendarium*, we tend to think of elves, men, dwarves, orcs (a.k.a. goblins), and hobbits as the "races" of Middle-earth. Other beings may or may not count as distinctive races: the Ainur, whether Vala or Maia, are angelic or god-like beings, which could be understood as its own race, particularly if we want to identify the race of Gandalf, Saruman, and Sauron. Along those lines, the great enemies, such as balrogs or dragons, could well be part of that race or could be set off as separate races. We are told in *The Silmarillion* that balrogs are maia (23), but it is less clear what class of being the dragons belong to; it is suggested that they were "bred" by Morgoth, yet they are clearly sentient, even wise, and it is an article of faith in Tolkien's universe that evil "can only mock, it cannot make: not real new things of its own," as Frodo tells Sam in *The Lord of the Rings* (*Return* 201). In *The Lord of the Rings*, Treebeard explains to Merry and Pippen that trolls are merely "counterfeits," made "in mockery of Ents, as Orcs were of Elves" (*Two Towers* 91), so trolls, along with the "stone giants" of *The Hobbit*, would appear to be a distinct race, like orcs are. Ents and ent-wives seem to be their own race, at least; they would not wish to be categorized with the trolls, certainly. Other "monsters" could be mentioned as well, such as the Watcher in the Water that lives in the lake by the western gates of Moria, or even Gollum, who is first encountered in *The Hobbit* as a unique monster, but who becomes somewhat humanized—or, rather, hobbitized—within *The Lord of the Rings*, as Gandalf surmises that Sméagol's people were likely distant relatives or even ancestors of hobbits of The Shire.

Then there are those categories of creatures who are not usually thought of as "races," such as animals. In *The Hobbit*, the word *race* is specifically applied to both eagles (104) and thrushes (228), or more particularly to a subset of each species, which suggests that Tolkien is using the term *race* in an older sense associated with kinship groups, as when he also has Thorin refer to "the race of Durin" (53, 192, 195), designating a line of descent *within* dwarf-kind, not dwarves in general. Similarly, Bard is "of the race of Dale," which explains why he can understand the language of the aforementioned thrush (250). Beorn, who is technically a man but who is also a werebear or skin-changer, may be a race unto himself; he becomes "a great chief" of a people known as the Beornings, and it was said that "the men of his line" could also take the form of a bear (296). Wolves, ravens, and other animals have both speech and personalities in the novel, which complicates matters further. But, for the most part, the concept of race remains normally associated with types of humanoid beings.

Good People and Decent Enough People

Delving deeply into the twelve-volume *History of Middle-earth*, Fimi characterizes the trajectory of Tolkien's career as moving "from fairies to hobbits," which does make for an elegant shorthand characterization. Hobbits, as we know, were somewhat accidental intruders into his imaginary history, and Tolkien's early passion was for what he initially called fairies, some of which became gnomes, and all of whom are best known to us as elves. In his famous letter to Milton Waldman, in which he offers a summary of his "Silmarillion" project—Christopher Tolkien later used a version of the letter as the preface to *The Silmarillion*, in fact—Tolkien takes pride in the fact that "the legendary *Silmarillion* is peculiar, and differs from all similar things I know in not being anthropocentric. Its centre of view and interest is not Men but 'Elves'" (*Letters* 147). He notes that "Men came in inevitably [...] But they remain peripheral—late comers, and however growingly important, not principals" (147). In Tolkien's mythology, the "first-born" elves are always the highest class of beings, but they are kindred to humans, the "second-born." Dwarves have a more complex history, but clearly they represent a similar type, and in *The Lord of the Rings*, Aragorn expressly speaks of "the Three Kindreds: Elves, Men, and Dwarves" (*Two Towers* 12). Hobbits, as we have seen, are not so much a distinct race as a subset of the human race, and the movement from fairies to hobbits in Tolkien's writing tied to the analogous movements from epic to novelistic literary forms and from a mythic to a historic mode of storytelling.

Tolkien's elves are distinctive, and differ greatly from the sort of fairy-tale elves of nursery rhymes. The elves in the trees singing "tra-la-la-lally" (48) as the Bilbo and the others enter Rivendell in *The Hobbit* (48) are probably not well suited to Tolkien's idea, although in their fundamental "goodness" they maintain their place in his hierarchical system. Tolkien wrote that, "of course, exterior to my story, Elves and Men are just different aspects of the Humane":

> The Elves represent, as it were, the artistic, aesthetic, and purely scientific aspects of the Humane nature raised to a higher level than is actually seen in Men. That is: they have a devoted love of the physical world and a desire to observe and understand it for its own sake and [...] not as a material for use or as a power-platform. They also possess a 'subcreational' or artistic faculty of great excellence. They are therefore 'immortal.' Not 'eternally,' but to endure with and within the created world, while its story lasts. (*Letters* 236)

In "Of Fairy-Stories," Tolkien corrects the false idea that elves are "supernatural," pointing out that "it is man who is, in contrast to fairies, supernatural [...]; whereas they are natural, far more natural than he. Such is their doom" (110). This view is, in part, based on Tolkien's Christianity, for mankind is "supernatural" in the sense that their spirits can leave the natural world, going to heaven or hell or wherever. In the "Silmarillion," this mysterious "doom of men" is seen as a blessing, a gift bestowed upon them by their creator, though some also lament it, for the elves, even in death, are doomed to remain part of the physical, natural world.

The superiority of the elves in the racial hierarchy of Middle-earth is closely related to Tolkien's sense that these "elvish" qualities in mankind are among the highest virtues. Hence, as with his implication of social class hierarchies, Tolkien's racial divisions are tied to matters of moral character—not that bigoted racists do not also justify racism in moral terms, of course, designating those they deem "inferior" as bad, evil, or otherwise worthy of contempt—rather than physical appearance or cultural difference, although these do seem to overlap in the racialism of Tolkien's world. For example, as I discuss in the next section, Tolkien's orcs (called "goblins" in *The Hobbit*) are literally demonized, imagined as a sort of demonic enemy, yet in his own characterization of that race, Tolkien emphasizes their contempt for the beautiful and the orderly, along with their cruelty and hard-heartedness. In wartime letters to his son Christopher, he makes reference to "orcs" frequently in a figurative sense, noting "I have met them, or thought so, in England's green and pleasant land" (90), and "we started with a great many Orcs on our side" (78); when Tolkien writes that Christopher is "a hobbit amongst the Urukhai" (78), the great orcs he refers to are Christopher's fellow English soldiers, not the ostensible enemies in "Deutschland or Nippon," countries in which there are probably "many such creatures" as well (90). Within his fiction, however, Tolkien takes an almost orc-like stance with respect to his orcs; although they are depicted as mostly human (all-too-human, perhaps), they are cruelly mistreated by the "good guys" at every turn. Tolkien was angered by the "gloating" of the English in their impending victory over the Germans, comparing their attitude to those who not only want to execute a criminal, but also "to gloat, or to hang his wife and child by him while the orc-crowd hooted" (*Letters* 111). As we see, many of Tolkien's heroes gloat over the deaths of orcs, but they never feel ashamed of themselves for doing so.

The elves in their moral and aesthetic supremacy are not without troubling attributes of their own. In *The Silmarillion*, following the cataclysmic war that ends the First Age, the elves who remained were urged to return to Valinor (i.e., the Undying Lands), but many chose to remain. As Tolkien puts it,

> There was nothing wrong essentially in their lingering against counsel [...] But they wanted to have their cake without eating it. They wanted the peace and bliss and perfect memory of "The West," and yet to remain on the ordinary earth where their prestige as the highest people, above wild Elves, dwarves, and Men, was greater than at the bottom of the hierarchy of Valinor. They thus became obsessed with "fading," the mode in which the changes of time (the law of the world under the sun) was perceived by them. (*Letters* 151)

The lure of "prestige as the highest people" must have been powerful. As we learn in *The Silmarillion*, "mightiest and fairest of all the Elves that remained" (358), Galadriel, had originally come to Middle-earth as an unabashed imperialist, "for she yearned to see the wide unguarded lands and to rule there a realm at her own will" (90). When readers meet her in *The Lord of the Rings*, she and her husband are ruling a land made up of "lesser" silvan elves (perhaps the kindred of the Elvenking's people), who presumably allowed their "betters" to govern them without resistance. The "natural order" requires that elves, the "high elves" within their own ranks and all elves with respect to other races, be atop the hierarchy.

In *The Hobbit*, a telling if simple example of the superiority of the elves comes from an expected moment during the Battle of Five Armies. As things are looking quite grim, Bilbo stands with the elves, "partly because there was more chance of escape from that point, but partly (with the more Tookish part of his mind) because if he was going to be in a last desperate stand, he preferred on the whole to defend the Elvenking" (286). It is understandable that Bilbo would not stand with the dwarves, since from Thorin's perspective he had betrayed them by taking the Arkenstone, but it is telling that Bilbo (or even the Tookish part of him) would prefer to defend the erstwhile enemy, one who was himself known to be avaricious, with a "weakness" for treasure ("though his hoard was rich, he was ever eager for more" [168]), and who had treated Bilbo's own friends badly and imprisoned them. Bilbo could have chosen to stand with the men of Lake-town who had treated him and his friends very well, for example. But Bilbo's natural inclination toward the elves, even ones as problematic as these former enemies, is itself a sign of the basic goodness of that race, for the reader is always positioned in such a way as to want to stand with Bilbo (and Gandalf) as well.

Elrond, whose father was a man and mother an elf, symbolizes the bridge between elves and men. He "was as noble and as fair in face as any elf-lord, as strong as a warrior, as wise as a wizard, as venerable as a king of the dwarves, and as kind as summer" (*Hobbit* 51). Elrond plays a role in all of Tolkien's tales, having witnessed the Fall of Gondolin in the First Age, fought Sauron in the War of the Last Alliance in the Second Age, and featuring prominently in the events of the Third Age, notably those depicted in *The Hobbit* and *The Lord of the Rings*. As we have seen, he represents lore and knowledge, drawing upon his own studies as well as vast experience and long memory. He helps to mark the transition from the Eldar Days (the epoch of elves) to our time.

The Age of Men might be, by definition, more *demotic*, but it is certainly not democratic, nor is there a sense of racial equality among men. In a memorable scene from *The Lord of the Rings*, Faramir offers a "Gondorian theory of anthropology" (as Virginia Luling has called it [54]): "For so we reckon Men in our lore, calling them the High, or Men of the West, which were Númenoreans; and the Middle Peoples, Men of the Twilight, such as are the Rohirrim and their kin that dwell still far in the North; and the Wild, the Men of Darkness" (*Two Towers* 323). This tripartite scheme reflects the one already established by the Elven order (i.e., the Light Elves who have lived in Valinor, the Middle ones who were delayed or stopped along the way, and the Wild "Avari" who never made the journey). The first Númenorean king was Elros, Elrond's brother who chose to be of the race of men (as Elrond chose to be an Elf), so the highest level of humankind is justified on the grounds that they biologically related to the elves. In a letter, Tolkien notes that Númenoreans "in appearance, and even in powers of mind" became "hardly distinguishable from the Elves," though they remained mortal (*Letters* 154). This intra-racial hierarchy reveals another thing, crucial to the geopolitical order within Middle-earth: Though the elves may depart or fade away, their hierarchy still determines who maintains the right and privilege to govern long after.

Bard, of *The Hobbit*, somewhat prefigures this system. Although he is a man of Lake-town, he is revealed to be of the line of Girion of Dale, and thus heir to the throne of that kingdom. (In any case, he is effectively named king by acclamation after slaying Smaug, so it works out nicely that he was already the heir.) Bard represents the heroic human, one fit to lead others, and to take his place at the end of the novel beside Elvenking and Dain, now King under the Mountain, as those races' respective leaders in that part of the world. To the extent that Bard stands out from other "men," the only other identified individual person is the feckless though canny, unnamed Master of Lake-town, and he represents the sinful side of man. Interestingly, the Master's is an elected position, so Lake-town is governed as a democracy, but this also means that the Master appears as a calculating politician, rather than some innately gifted leader. (As Tolkien had said, he is not himself a democrat, and the democratic values of Lake-town are not necessarily presented as virtuous; the old Master is a villain, and at the end of the novel Balin mentions that "[t]he new Master is of wiser kind […] and very popular; for, of course, he gets most of the credit for the present prosperity" [305], which is perhaps meant ironically as well.) Otherwise, we meet very few humans in *The Hobbit*. Apart from Beorn, who is unique, most of the other humans remain "extras" in the background or are mentioned only in passing.

A hobbit is the "hero" of the novel, but nearly every chapter of Bilbo's narrative features dwarves, which makes that "race" rather prominent in the story. Over 200 pages into *The Hobbit*, there is an extraordinary paragraph in which the race of dwarves as a whole is given a rather broad-brushed character. Having gained entry into the Lonely Mountain through the secret door, Thorin now sends Bilbo to investigate the interior while the rest of the dwarves wait. The implication that they are forcing Bilbo to perform dangerous work alone and unaided leads to a tacit condemnation, for, as the narrator puts it,

> The most that can be said for the dwarves is this: they intended to pay
> Bilbo really handsomely for his services; they had brought him to do a
> nasty job for them, and the did not mind the poor fellow doing it if he
> would; but they would all have done their best to get him out of trouble,
> if he got into to it, as they did in the case of the trolls at the beginning
> of their adventures before they had particular reasons for being grateful
> to him. There it is: dwarves are not heroes, but calculating folk with a
> great idea of the value of money; some are tricky and treacherous and
> pretty bad lots; some are not, but are decent enough people like Thorin
> and Company, if you don't expect too much. (213)

The "most that can be said for the dwarves" is rather striking, all the
more so given its location in the text. Had it been mentioned during the
first chapter, when a flummoxed Bilbo was encountering an unexpected
party of strange dwarves, it may have served to characterize his own views
about this race of people by making what could seem to be rudeness
appear more like a quirky character trait. But the phrase appears more
than two-thirds of the way through the novel, long after Bilbo and the
dwarves have shared many hardships and adventures, as well as good
times, and have gotten to know (and like) each other fairly well.

Moreover, the comment about "decent enough people" comes well
after the earlier revelation that all elves, even ones "more dangerous and
less wise" than others, are "good people," and the distinction between
"good" and "decent enough" is quite clear. Elves are inherently good, and
goblins inherently bad, but one cannot easily determine the goodness of a
dwarf in Tolkien's *legendarium*, even in a story featuring thirteen dwarves
as protagonists. Indeed, the fact that only "some" dwarves, including
Thorin and Company, are *not* "tricky and treacherous and pretty bad
lots" suggest that even being "decent enough people" is not necessarily
the norm for that race. Of course, by the end, Bilbo is reconciled with
Thorin, Dain is a great hero and leader, and dwarves in general are
restored to the side of the "good," but the sense of them as a race
apart, one not always to be trusted—the perpetual mistrust between the
always "good" elves and dwarves does not speak well of the dwarves, after
all—persists.

Tolkien has compared the dwarves as a people to the Jews, and
there has always been some discomfort in the ways Tolkien's work

exhibits potentially anti-Semitic attitudes with respect to them. Those who defend Tolkien most strenuously against charges of anti-Semitism (or of racism more generally) almost always cite his 1938 letter, written in response to an inquiry by the publisher of the German translation of *The Hobbit* about Tolkien's own origins, specifically wondering whether the name might be Jewish. His angry, impassioned response, in which he writes "I can only reply that I regret that I appear to have *no* ancestors of that gifted people" (37), registers his hatred of the Hitler program (elsewhere he refers to the man himself as a "ruddy little ignoramus" [55]), and perhaps even indicates a level of philo-Semitism. However, as Stuart observes, such "philo-Semitism is just as racist as anti-Semitism, in that it ranks races hierarchically" (237); in fact, a "word like 'gifted' is, by definition, comparative and hierarchical," and so "there must have been, in Tolkien's estimation, peoples not as 'gifted' as the Jews" (237–238). Of his own depictions of them in his tales, Tolkien wrote that "I do think of the 'Dwarves' like Jews: at once native and alien in their habitations, speaking the languages of the country, but with an accent due to their own private tongue" (*Letters* 229). The characterization of the dwarves as a people exiled from their homeland comports well with the plot of *The Hobbit*, where Thorin seeks to reclaim his ancestral home from the invader to drove his people out, but Tolkien also seems to imagine the dwarves as a race as being *essentially* diasporic. Their lack of a "home" within Middle-earth, arguably, implies a lack of belonging as well, which is troubling.

If the truly heroic can be found only among elves and men, for dwarves are characterized by Tolkien for the most part as being too limited in their worldview and their capabilities to be "heroes" (except, perhaps, for Gimli in *The Lord of the Rings*, the only "elf-friend" of his kind), then the hobbits are in effect ennobled by their non-heroic status. They are "lesser men" in nearly every possible imagining of the term, yet for Tolkien they become the creatures who redeem the world of men, "putting earth under the feet of 'romance'" (*Letters* 215), and establishing simplicity itself as a virtue. Thorin's dying words uttered to Bilbo serve as a kind of motto for this philosophy—"If more of us valued food and cheer and song above hoarded gold, it would be a merrier world" (290)—but Bilbo's own simple heroism establishes the broader view that, as Tolkien insisted, "'the wheels of the world,' are often turned not by Lords and Governors, even gods, but by the seemingly unknown and weak" (*Letters* 149). The status of hobbits as "lesser" men, who in their simplicity may lack some of the baleful attributes of seemingly "great men," in the end helps to assure that the best of them remain not just decent enough, but good people.

Cruel, Wicked, and Bad-Hearted

There are many monsters in Tolkien's world, along with numerous animals viewed as enemies and a few individuals who are considered truly bad, not least of whom is Smaug the dragon, but arguably there is only one race that is evil. In *The Hobbit*, they named *goblins*, but in the rest of Tolkien's *legendarium*, the term *orcs* is preferred. The goblins serve as the enemy of nearly all "good" people, and quite unlike other military or moral adversaries, they are shown no mercy whatsoever by the heroes in Tolkien's work. As Shippey has put it, "Orcs entered Middle-earth originally just because the story needed a continual supply of enemies over whom one need feel no compunction" (*Road* 233), but given what Tolkien reveals about this race, their cultures, and even various personalities, such lack of concern for them is quite disturbing. Even Tolkien himself expressed reservations about the impression that orcs were "irredeemably" evil, which violated his own religious views and the underlying morality of his imagined universe, for "God" (or Eru Ilúvatar in the mythology) had clearly allowed these sentient beings to exist in the first place. As Tolkien put it, "by accepting or tolerating their making—necessary to their actual existence—even Orcs would become part of the World, which is God's and ultimately good" (*Letters* 195). And yet, in Tolkien's entire *oeuvre*, it seems, the only "good orc" is a dead orc.

Tolkien's uneasiness about the moral standing of this race caused enough concern that he toyed with different origin stories to account for the existence of orcs. The canonical view is that the elves, "by slow arts of cruelty were corrupted and enslaved; thus did Melkor breed the hideous race of the Orcs in envy and mockery of the Elves" (*Silmarillion* 47). Elsewhere in *The Silmarillion*, the surmise that orcs were former elves—specifically the Avari or Dark Elves, who did not make the long journey to Valinor as did the Light Elves—is given credence: "Whence they [the orcs] came, or what they were, the Elves knew not then, thinking them perhaps to be Avari who had become evil and savage in the wild; in which they guessed all too near, it is said" (103–104). This explanation would make the most sense in Tolkien's *legendarium*, if only because orcs appear after elves but before men in the mythic history of Arda. However, as Fimi points out, "the thought that the hideous and malicious Orcs were once Elves—the 'highest' beings of Middle-earth—became increasingly unbearable to Tolkien" (155). Thus, in unpublished manuscripts written during the 1950s and 1960s Tolkien toyed with several different ideas to explain the orcs' existence, ranging from corrupted men (rather than corrupted elves) to low-level Maia (and hence, fallen "angels" like Sauron himself) or even automata without reason who were essentially puppets controlled by Morgoth or Sauron, an admittedly unlikely scenario (see *Morgoth's Ring* 408–425). There is also the vague suggestion that orcs *were* a kind of man, distant cousins of the Drúedain or related to the Púkel Men who appear in *The Lord of the Rings*: "some thought, nonetheless, that there had been a remote kinship, which accounted for their special enmity. Orcs and Drûgs each regarded the other as renegades" (*Unfinished Tales* 401–402). Ultimately, as Christopher Tolkien concludes, "[t]his would appear to be my father's final view on the matter: Orcs were bred from Men" (*Morgoth's Ring* 421).

Tolkien was explicit when it came to the "human" appearance of orcs, and while *The Hobbit* does not describe their physical attributes, in *The Lord of the Rings* their features are mentioned frequently, and one can only read about the "swart," "sallow-skinned," and "slant-eyed" orcs so many times without becoming offended. In a letter, Tolkien himself invites a racial characterization of orcs: "Orcs are definitely stated to be corruptions of the 'human' form seen in Elves and Men. They are (or were) squat, broad, flat-nosed, sallow-skinned, with wide mouths and slant eyes: in fact degraded and repulsive versions of the (to Europeans) least lovely Mongol-type" (*Letters* 274). Demonizing of the enemy is common enough in wartime, part of the "gross dichotomizing" Paul Fussell discusses in his great history of the first World War (see Fussell 75; see also Croft 47–50). Here, as elsewhere, the enmonstering of the adversary has distinctively racial and racist character.

Culturally, the goblins in *The Hobbit* are as "advanced" (a term Tolkien refers to ironically) as any other race. "They make no beautiful things, but they make many clever ones," and the narrator speculates that "[i]t is not unlikely that they invented some of the machines that have since troubled the world, especially ingenious devices for killing large numbers of people at once" (62). (I would point out that the only time in *The Hobbit* in which we see numbers of people killed "at once" is when Gandalf kills goblins in the Misty Mountain cave, leaving behind "a smell like gunpower" [60], before later setting fire to goblins and wargs in great numbers.) Apparently, goblins "hated everybody and everything, and particularly the orderly and prosperous," but "in some parts wicked dwarves had even made alliances with them" (62), a reference that seems to damn the dwarven race by association. The goblins are described as being "cruel, wicked, and bad-hearted," but apart from also being "usually being untidy" (62), the goblins appear to be part of a relatively stable, self-governing, and well organized civilization.

Even in their simplified presentation in *The Hobbit*, the goblins appear quite human, if not always humane. The goblins who capture Bilbo and the dwarves in the Misty Mountains clearly have a social order, with a sense of law and order. Notably, they manage to take prisoners alive and unharmed for questioning, while Gandalf immediately kills "several" goblins without a thought for the value of their lives. In the previous chapter, Thorin had graciously accepted from Elrond the sword whose name meant "Goblin-cleaver," saying "May it soon cleave goblins once again!" (52). So, when the Great Goblin wonders whether Thorin and his companions constitute "[m]urderers and friends of Elves, not unlikely" (63), he guesses aright, mostly. In fact, during his interrogation of Thorin, the Great Goblin is no more impertinent than the "good" Elvenking, who treats Thorin and Balin almost as badly in questioning them after forcibly arresting them for a similar "crime" (i.e., trespassing; the word "crime" is used by the Elvenking [173]). Although goblins are depicted as being inherently evil, they clearly maintain a moral code that aligns with that of elves, men, and dwarves, for the most part; that is, they do not, like Milton's Satan, reverse the ethical poles ("Evil, be thou my Good"), but follow the standard view in which crimes like murder and theft ought to be punished, lying is immoral, and disloyalty is a sign of bad faith. As Shippey has put it, referring to a scene in *The Lord of the Rings*, "Orcs here, and on other occasions, have a clear idea of what is admirable and what is contemptible behavior, which is exactly the same as ours" (*J.R.R. Tolkien* 133). A race that was *inherently* evil would probably not share their ethical and legal value-systems with the "good people" of Middle-earth.

Quite unlike the parallel scene in which the Elvenking interrogates the dwarves, the Great Goblin is killed only seconds after he begins questioning the suspects, and before Gandalf stabs him, the wizard effectively sets fire to all the goblins in the room, as his "piercing white sparks" were "burning holes into the goblins," whose screams of pain were so horrifying that "[s]everal hundred wild cats and wolves being roasted slowly alive together would not have compared with it" (64). The abject cruelty of this act by Gandalf is astonishing, as is his laughter in recounting the story (96). It may be that an escape was necessary, as with the trolls before and the spiders (not to mention the elves) later, but the savage delight with which goblins are violently murdered is hard to ignore. Worse still, perhaps, is the only reference in Tolkien's entire body of writings to a goblin (or orc) ever being captured for questioning, even though there are a number of instances, as in the scene from *The Hobbit*, in which orcs keep their own captives alive. Beorn reveals that he had captured a goblin and a warg, from whom he learned of the attacks on the Great Goblin, the warg chief, and "the death from the wizard's fire of many" others. Beorn "chuckled fiercely to himself" as he relates the story, and when Bilbo asks him what became of Beorn's captives, he shows them: "[a] goblin's head was stuck outside the gate and a warg's skin was nailed to a tree just beyond" (131).

Had Tolkien wished to create simple monsters, demonic figures who were inherently evil, it would not have been difficult to do so. Tolkien strengths in world-building and his devoting myth-making undoubtedly prevented him from relying on such one-dimensional enemies, which is why the treatment of them by the "heroes" becomes so disturbing.

Tolkien obviously provides more ethnographic and cultural background for goblins than a mere plot-device would require. The orcs or goblins of Middle-earth are shown to have their own languages, customs, communities, and even families. In *The Hobbit*, for instance, Gandalf declares, "[t]he Goblins are upon you! Bolg of the North is coming, O Dain! whose father you slew in Moria" (281), and the actual battle in which Bolg's father, Azog, is killed by Dáin Ironfoot is described in Appendix A to *The Lord of the Rings* (*Return of the King* 392). Vengeance and familial honor motivate the assault, more so than some inherently "evil" nature, and the attack by the goblins of Gundabad—a rare, named "capital" of a civilization—was further motivated by the need to answer the killing of the Great Goblin. Vengefulness is not a virtue, but it is undoubtedly an understandable, human impulse, one that the elves, men, and dwarves know all too well from their own experience. After the victory of the "good" people in the Battle of Five Armies, the remaining goblins become fugitives, but most are hunted down and killed before they can escape. Needless to say, there are no prisoners of war, no amnesty, and no mercy shown to the defeated, retreating soldiers. Although the precise numbers are not available, "[s]ongs have said that three parts of the goblin warriors of the North perished on that day" (292).

Ultimately, the "evil" of goblins and the mercilessness with which goblins are treated are problems for *The Hobbit* and for Tolkien's work more generally, but this case might offer an instructive example of racism *within* Tolkien's world. The goblins' physical and cultural similarity to elves, humans, and dwarves, not to mention their right to exist as "rational, incarnate beings" (*Letters* 195), suggests that the unthinking demonization of the entire race by elves, humans, and most dwarves stems, at least in part, from what Freud famously called "the narcissism of minor differences" (*Civilization* 72). The geopolitical order of Middle-earth has no "good" or "evil" peoples, but as in our own world system, there will be no shortage of people who will divide cultures and societies along such artificial lines, and some who will be happy to do so using "race" as a shorthand for such moralizing, with the dehumanizing violence that inevitably accompanies it. Reading *The Hobbit* "against the grain," to use a famous expression from Walter Benjamin, we might see the goblins as a race whose demonization calls into question the stability and hierarchy of the other races, ultimately allowing us to discard such racial characterizations entirely, in order to focus attention on more foundational, underlying evils at work.

Dragon Sickness

If there is a clearly hierarchical system in Tolkien's world when it comes to race, there is a less visible but still noteworthy social structure built upon relations of social and economic class. These are often indirectly related to the questions of racial hierarchy, since wealth tends to accrue along the same lines, and within races, groups with the most wealth tend to be the most important, even morally elevated above the other, "lesser" folk. Throughout *The Hobbit*, signs of wealth are usually taken as signs of worth, even if Tolkien also tempers this sentiment with a critique of greed. Nevertheless, as we have seen, some expressly greedy characters— the Elvenking, for one—are still held in high regard, whereas others, like the Master of Lake-town, are condemned for it.

Avarice, more than any other evil, seems to be the ultimate moral failing in *The Hobbit*. The narrative's main quest itself involves the attempt to defeat what might be considered the very avatar of that vice, a dragon, which is a creature known for lusting after and hoarding gold, gems, and other treasures. The term "dragon-sickness" is used only once, in reference to the old Master of Lake-town who succumbed to this "disease," which eventually led to his death "by starvation in the Waste, deserted by his companions" (305), although the illness seemed to have infected Thorin as well, all the more susceptible in the narrator's view because of his "dwarvish heart" perhaps (265), and Bilbo himself was "in grievous danger of coming under the dragon-spell" earlier (224). The Elvenking might have been immune, but "[i]f the elf-king had a weakness it was for treasure, especially for silver and white gems" (168). Trolls and goblins, apparently defined by their rapaciousness, are also at risk. Even the Sackville-Bagginses, hobbits of The Shire, seem to be afflicted, enough so to covet (and to pocket) Bilbo's silver spoons! (303). Wealth, not to mention the power over others that accompanies it, lies at the heart of the conflicts that typify the geopolitics of Middle-earth in this period, which is ultimately what makes Bilbo, who is literally a "lesser" member of the human race, the hero.

On the first page of *The Hobbit*, readers learn that Bilbo Baggins is "a very well-to-do hobbit," which makes things easier for the narrative as a whole, but crucial to Bilbo's "good" character is that he is not greedy, either for money or power. He shows little interest in his "fourteenth share" of the treasure, due to him by contractual obligation, and he even tries to give away the treasure he had taken from the trolls' cache (301). Bilbo lacks for very little, before or after his journey, but he also desires no more than he needs. Bourgeois he may be, in terms of his middling if comfortable social class, but acquisitive he is not. In the end, Tolkien's model for the non-heroic hero is just an ordinarily fellow, doing what he thinks is best, mostly because he has little other choice.

Desire for power over others, even if that desire includes the motivation to do "good," is the ultimate evil in Tolkien's *legendarium*, one that is fully on display across his racial divides. Countering such desire without succumbing to it oneself, as the example of Bilbo demonstrates, is the ultimate quest.

6

Conclusion: *Quite a Little Fellow in a Wide World*

In Bertolt Brecht's *Life of Galileo*, a play written shortly after *The Hobbit* first appeared in print, a passionate, idealistic character laments "Unhappy the land that has no heroes," to which a weary Galileo responds, "No, unhappy the land that needs heroes."

Tolkien's politics are not Brecht's, far from it, and neither are his aesthetics, but from their completely different perspectives both writers were skeptical of the heroism and hero-worship so pervasive in modern culture. This judgment likely sounds perverse to many readers, for Tolkien was himself a lover of "heroic romance," to name the generic label he applied to *The Lord of the Rings* (see *Letters* 414), and he had said that a "basic passion of mine *ab initio* was for myth [...] and for fairy-story, and above all for heroic legend on the brink of fairy-story and history," which "were not divergent interests—opposite poles of science and romance—but integrally related" (*Letters* 144). Tolkien's *legendarium* contains many heroes, in fact, and the tales of some, such as Beren and Lúthien, reverberate throughout the ages of Middle-earth. However, just as Sam Gamgee comes to realize in *The Lord of the Rings* that he and Frodo are themselves taking part in the ongoing story of Beren and

© The Author(s), under exclusive license to Springer Nature Switzerland AG 2022
R. T. Tally Jr., *J. R. R. Tolkien's* The Hobbit,
Palgrave Science Fiction and Fantasy: A New Canon,
https://doi.org/10.1007/978-3-031-11266-9_6

Lúthien, marveling "Don't the great stories never end?" (*Two Towers* 353) and thus becoming aware of his place in the grand narrative of history, the reader of Tolkien's work comes to recognize that the armature of the heroic romance may be used for stories that, perhaps paradoxically, disclose the value of "ordinary" people in making history. *The Hobbit* is fundamentally a tale of the anti-heroic heroism to be found in regular people's efforts to deal with the exigencies of their time.

Early in the novel, as the dwarves are discussing strategies for entering the Lonely Mountain and dealing with the dragon there, Gandalf notes that they could not enter through the main gate, "not without a Warrior, even a Hero. I tried to find one; but warriors are busy fighting one another in distant lands, and in this neighborhood heroes are scarce, or simply not to be found. [...] That is why I settled on *burglary*" (21–22). Bilbo is thus designated as the non-hero best suited for this mission, but Gandalf's comment on the availability of warriors and heroes can also seem strikingly apt for those of us who live in a world of perpetual warfare but that lacks for heroes worthy of the name. Marx's famous rhetorical question, "is Achilles possible in an era of powder and lead?" is not merely a comment on the technology of weaponry or even of print, but concerns a more fundamental break between the pre-capitalist social formations and our own modern ones in which the "necessary conditions of epic poetry vanish" (*Grundrisse* 111). As in Lukács's *Theory of the Novel*, in which "the epic and the novel [...] differ from one another not by their authors' fundamental intentions but by the given historico-philosophical realities with which the authors were confronted" (56), the era of the bourgeoisie is not suited the epic or even tragic hero, but to the ordinary persons who find themselves in extraordinary situations.

In a scene from *The Lord of the Rings* that has been given whole new life in our own "dark times," Frodo expresses his wish that these horrific circumstances had not happened in his lifetime, and Gandalf responds, "So do I, and so do all who live to see such times. But that is not for them to decide. All we have to decide is what to do with the time that is given us" (*Fellowship* 55–56). Although that novel features heroes and heroism, Tolkien makes sure to let us know that the hobbits are still at the heart of the story, and indeed, Sam—the lone "working-class" hobbit, least worldly and most humble of the protagonists—is perhaps the ultimate "hero" of the tale. Moreover, it is important to remember that Gollum, quite possibly the most unlikely of all potentially "heroic" characters, is the one who actually destroys the ring, thus making possible the post-War of the Ring epoch.

Despite the grandeur of its epic traditions, Tolkien's work in the end embraces an attitude closer to those who have urged us to see "history from below," which may be all the more fitting for a series of stories that began with a character who lived in a hole in the ground. The sense of Tolkien as devoutly religious, vaguely anarchistic, and culturally conservative is, of course, no impediment to interpreting the ideas to be found in his writings in a more radical way, for Tolkien's desire for narrative—a desire Fredric Jameson, following Jean-François Lyotard, characterized as the "desire called Marx"—reveals his project of restoring the historical consciousness to the modern world, which in turn fosters a revisionary mode of interpretation. The idea of *history from below* is quite old, of course, but the term is sometimes credited to the historian Lucian Febvre, co-founder of the *Annales* school of historiography, who referred to *histoire de masses et non vedettes, histoire vue d'en bas et non d'en haut* ("history of the masses and not the stars, history viewed from below and not from on high" [576]). As a slogan, it was probably best established by the Marxist historian E. P. Thompson in a 1966 article titled "History from Below" in the *Times Literary Supplement*, and then popularized further by Howard Zinn's *A People's History of the United States* (1980). These socialists held rather different political views than Tolkien, naturally, but then both politics and art can make for strange bedfellows. After all, Marx's favorite writer, after Shakespeare, was Honoré de Balzac, a reactionary royalist bourgeois. Further, Tolkien's own religious convictions, while nominally conservative, can be evaluated in terms of more secular figurations. Thus, when defending of his seemingly democratic vision of the ordinary man as the real hero of history, Tolkien writes, "Not that I am a 'democrat' in any of its current uses; except that I suppose, to speak in literary terms, we are all equal before the Great Author, *qui deposuit potentes de sede et exaltavit humiles* ['who has put down the powerful from their seat and raised up the humble']" (*Letters* 215). Tolkien refers here to God, but we may also see in his imagination the figuring forth of a world system, "which is for us the absent totality, Spinoza's God or Nature, the ultimate (indeed, perhaps the only) referent, the true ground of Being of our own time," as Jameson has put it in *The Geopolitical Aesthetic* (82): or, in other words, History, whose ruses or dialectical reversals are revealed to turn worlds upside down again and again.

In *The Lord of the Rings*, Elrond—a character whose very presence embodies the grand traditions of fairy stories and heroic legends—is the one who acknowledges both the fact and the wisdom of viewing history from below, as it were. During the Council of Elrond, he states, "such is oft the course of deeds that move the wheels of the world: small hands do them because they must, while the eyes of the great are elsewhere" (*Fellowship* 302). Understandably, readers tend to place emphasis on the "small hands," and Bilbo even takes it as a hint that Elrond means for him to do the job himself, but just as significant is the "because they must" clause, which harkens back to Frodo's decision over what to do in the time given to him. Small hands do not turn the wheels of the world because they are trying to be furtive or heroic, but merely because they are doing whatever seems to need to be done at that time. Beyond the most limited ones, the outcomes and ramifications of such deeds are always unknown, for "even the very wise cannot see all ends" (*Fellowship* 65), and much that seemed prudent might turn out for the worst, which is another reason to be wary of "heroes" who self-consciously and over-confidently view their own actions as inherently noble or good. Muddling through as best as one can, with little knowledge of the ultimate result, is evidently the human condition, but it is also what makes history.

This observation discloses a key element of Tolkien's philosophy of history and of what he calls "world-politics." The "value of Hobbits," as Tolkien informed W. H. Auden, lay "in putting earth under the feet of 'romance,' and in providing subjects for 'ennoblement' and heroes more praiseworthy than the professionals." Tolkien then adds, "*nolo heroizari* is as good a start for a hero, as *nolo espiscopari* for a bishop" (*Letters* 215). Referring to the traditional Church requirement that a person to be appointed bishop should refuse it ("I do not wish to be a bishop"), Tolkien maintains that the only heroes worthy of the role are those who do not wish to be heroes, and, in any case, anyone cast in the role of a hero must be modest when assessing goals and accomplishments. Gandalf reminds us that, even as we may recognize the heroism of hobbits like Bilbo, "only a small part is played in great deeds by any hero" (*Fellowship* 303).

Hence, in a novel that begins with a person living in a hole in the ground we find great deeds and events of world-historical significance, an elaborate and diverse array of landscapes and territories, and a direct link between our own world and the mist-enveloped regions of the distant past, the "hero" is last seen cheerfully acknowledging the smallness of his place in that grand narrative and world system. *The Hobbit* starts with the wandering wizard Gandalf the Grey "looking for someone to share in an adventure I am arranging," as he tells Bilbo Baggins, who responds that hobbits "have no use for adventures. Nasty disturbing uncomfortable things! Make you late for dinner!" (4); the meeting is merely a prelude to an adventure in which the bourgeois Bilbo leaves the comforts of home, travels over hill and under hill, across rivers, valleys, forests, mountains, and lakes, all while accompanying dwarves and encountering trolls, elves, goblins, Gollum, wolves, eagles, a werebear, giant spiders, more elves, lake-men, and, of course, a dragon, not to mention a "world war" writ small. But, after all of these escapades, the final scene of novel portrays Bilbo sitting with Gandalf and Balin in his cozy little home at Bag-End, sharing the tobacco-jar with the wizard, who tells him that, notwithstanding the role he has played in shaping some of the epochal, transformative events of the Third Age of Middle-earth, "You are a very fine person, Mr. Baggins, and I am very fond of you; but you are only quite a little fellow in the wide world after all," to which Bilbo assents: "Thank goodness!" (305).

Toward the end of Brecht's *Galileo*, the same former student who had condemned his teacher for not being a hero in a land that needed one changes his mind, realizing the Galileo's refusal to become a martyr actually was a heroic decision, for it had allowed him to continue doing scientific research and thus to bring into being the new world that modern science would make knowable. But again, Galileo corrects him, saying that his decision had nothing to do with any of that, but merely with the simpler desire to evade pain and torment, an altogether human concern. The putatively heroic acts of Bilbo Baggins are mostly performed in the service of avoiding pain, for himself and others, and largely involve faltering efforts in the dark, supplemented by chance or luck, amid forces far beyond his control or even knowledge. It is the situation of the subject in history, who cannot help but to make that history even while being formed by it. That it takes place in a "fantasy" world in no way diminishes its effectiveness, for as China Miéville has asserted, "we need fantasy to think the world, and to change it." ("Introduction" 48). Tolkien's great historical novel, *The Hobbit*, is classic work of fantasy and a monument to historical awareness, one that can help us even now to think our own world anew and, possibly, to imagine alternatives.

Bibliography

This bibliography lists works cited in this study, along with a limited selection of other books and articles, but it is in no way intended to be seen as comprehensive or even as an adequate representation of the field of Tolkien Studies. The wealth of scholarly and critical writing on J. R. R. Tolkien's life and work exceeds that of any dragon's hoard, and it grows daily as both specialists and generalists alike, scholars, critics, and fans, continue to contribute to its literary treasury. (For example, to cite just one of my favorite journals in the field, *Mythlore* makes available on its website an index of all the articles it has published, and at last check that index was 419 pages long.) By listing any texts at all, I commit the offense of not listing many other important works, and so I encourage all readers to explore the libraries, periodicals, scholarly societies, fan outlets, and other resources available to them, which like the roads, go ever ever on.

© The Editor(s) (if applicable) and The Author(s), under exclusive
license to Springer Nature Switzerland AG 2022
R. T. Tally Jr., *J. R. R. Tolkien's* The Hobbit,
Palgrave Science Fiction and Fantasy: A New Canon,
https://doi.org/10.1007/978-3-031-11266-9

Selected Works by J. R. R. Tolkien

Beowulf: A Translation and Commentary. Ed. Christopher Tolkien. Houghton Mifflin, 2014.

"*Beowulf*: The Monsters and the Critics." *The Monsters and the Critics and Other Essays*. Edited by Christopher Tolkien. HarperCollins, 1983. 5–48.

The History of Middle-earth (12 volumes)

The Book of Lost Tales, Part I. Ed. Christopher Tolkien. *The History of Middle-earth*: Vol. 1. George Allen and Unwin, 1983.

The Book of Lost Tales, Part II. Ed. Christopher Tolkien. *The History of Middle-earth*: Vol. 2. George Allen and Unwin, 1984.

The Lays of Beleriand. Ed. Christopher Tolkien. *The History of Middle-earth*: Vol. 3. George Allen and Unwin, 1985.

The Shaping of Middle-earth. Ed. Christopher Tolkien. *The History of Middle-earth*: Vol. 4. George Allen and Unwin, 1986.

The Lost Road and Other Writings. Ed. Christopher Tolkien. *The History of Middle-earth*: Vol. 5. Unwin Hyman, 1987.

The Return of the Shadow. Ed. Christopher Tolkien. *The History of Middle-earth*: Vol. 6. Unwin Hyman, 1988.

The Treason of Isengard. Ed. Christopher Tolkien. *The History of Middle-earth*: Vol. 7. Unwin Hyman, 1989.

The War of the Ring. Ed. Christopher Tolkien. *The History of Middle-earth*: Vol. 8. Unwin Hyman, 1990.

Sauron Defeated. Ed. Christopher Tolkien. *The History of Middle-earth*: Vol. 9. HarperCollins, 1992.

Morgoth's Ring. Ed. Christopher Tolkien. *The History of Middle-earth*: Vol. 10. HarperCollins, 1993.

The War of the Jewels. Ed. Christopher Tolkien. *The History of Middle-earth*: Vol. 11. HarperCollins, 1994.

The Peoples of Middle-earth. Ed. Christopher Tolkien. *The History of Middle-earth*: Vol. 12. HarperCollins, 1996.

The Hobbit. Del Rey, 1982.

"Leaf By Niggle." *The Tolkien Reader*. Del Rey, 1966. 100–120.

The Letters of J. R. R. Tolkien. Ed. Humphrey Carpenter. Houghton Mifflin, 1981.

The Lord of the Rings (in three volumes)

The Fellowship of the Ring. Del Rey, 1965.

The Two Towers. Del Rey, 1965.

The Return of the King. Del Rey, 1965.

"Mythopoiea." *Tree and Leaf*. HarperCollins, 2001. 85–90.

"On Fairy-Stories." *The Monsters and the Critics and Other Essays*. Edited by Christopher Tolkien. HarperCollins, 1983. 109–161.

The Silmarillion. Del Rey, 1977.

Unfinished Tales of Númenor and Middle-earth. Ed. Christopher Tolkien. Del Rey, 1988.

Works Cited

Althusser, Louis. "Ideology and Ideological State Apparatuses (Notes Toward an Investigation). " *Lenin and Philosophy and Other Essays*. Trans. Ben Brewster. Monthly Review Press, 1971. 127–186.

Anderson, Douglas A., ed. *The Annotated Hobbit*. 2nd ed. Boston: Houghton Mifflin, 2002.

Aristotle. *The Poetics*. Trans. S.H. Butcher. Hill and Wang, 1961.

Atwood, Margaret. *Alias Grace*. Anchor Books, 1996.

Bakhtin, Mikhail. *The Dialogic Imagination: Four Essays*. Edited and translated by Caryl Emerson and Michael Holquist. U of Texas P, 1981.

Bates, Brian. *The Real Middle-earth: Exploring the Magic and Mystery of the Middle Ages, J.R.R. Tolkien, and* The Lord of the Rings. Palgrave Macmillan, 2003.

Booth, Wayne. *The Rhetoric of Fiction*. 2nd ed. U of Chicago P, 1983.

Brecht, Bertolt. *Galileo*. Trans. Charles Laughton. Grove Press, 1966.

Carpenter, Humphrey. *J. R. R. Tolkien: A Biography*. Houghton Mifflin, 2000.

———. *The Inklings: C.S. Lewis, J.R.R. Tolkien, Charles Williams, and Their Friends*. HarperCollins, 2006.

Certeau, Michel de. *The Practice of Everyday Life*. Trans. Steven Rendall. U of California P, 1984.

Chance, Jane. "Subversive Fantasist: Tolkien on Class Difference." In *The Lord of the Rings, 1954 –2004: Scholarship in Honor of Richard E. Blackwelder*. Eds. Wayne Hammond and Cristina Scull. Marquette UP, 2006. 153–168.

Chance, Jane, and Alfred K. Siewers, eds. *Tolkien's Modern Middle Ages*. Palgrave Macmillan, 2005.

Conley, Tom. "*The Lord of the Rings* and the Fellowship of the Map." In *From Hobbits to Hollywood: Essays on Peter Jackson's* Lord of the Rings. Eds. Earnest Mathijs and Murray Pomerance. Rodopi, 2006. 215–229.

Croft, Janet Brennan. *War in the Works of J.R.R. Tolkien*. Praeger, 2004.

Croft, Janet Brenan, and Leslie A. Donovan, eds. *Perilous and Fair: Women in the Works and Life of J. R. R. Tolkien.* Mythopoeic Press, 2015.

Ekman, Stefan. *Here Be Dragons: Exploring Fantasy Maps and Settings.* Middletown, Connecticut: Wesleyan University Press, 2013.

Ellmann, Mary. "Growing Up Hobbitic." *New American Review* 2 (1968): 217–229.

Febvre, Lucien. "Albert Mathiez: Un tempérament, une education." *Annales d'histoire économique et sociale* 18 (November 1932): 573–576.

Fimi, Dimitra. *Tolkien, Race, and Cultural History: From Fairies to Hobbits.* Palgrave Macmillan, 2009.

Firchow, Peter E. "The Politics of Fantasy: *The Hobbit* and Fascism." *Midwest Quarterly* 51.1 (Autumn 2008): 15–27.

Flieger, Verlyn. "A Postmodern Medievalist?" In *Tolkien's Modern Middle Ages.* Eds. Jane Chance and Alfred K. Siewers. Palgrave Macmillan, 2005. 17–28.

———. *A Question of Time: J. R. R. Tolkien's Road to* Faërie. Kent State UP, 1997.

———. *There Would Always Be a Fairy Tale: More Essays on Tolkien.* Kent State UP, 2017.

Fonstad, Karen Wynn. *The Atlas of Middle-earth.* Rev. ed. Houghton Mifflin, 1991.

Freud, Sigmund. *Civilization and Its Discontents.* Trans. James Strachey. W.W. Norton, 1989.

Fussell, Paul. *The Great War and Modern Memory.* 25th Anniversary edition. Oxford UP, 2000.

Garth, John. *The Worlds of J. R. R. Tolkien: The Places That Inspired Middle-earth.* Princeton UP, 2020.

———. *The Worlds of J.R.R. Tolkien: The Places that Inspired Middle-earth.* Princeton UP, 2020.

Houghton, John Wm., Janet Brennan Croft, Nancy Martsch, John D. Rateliff, and Robin Anne Reid, eds. *Tolkien in the New Century: Essays in Honor of Tom Shippey.* McFarland & Company, 2014.

Hume, Kathryn. *Fantasy and Mimesis: Responses to Reality in Western Literature.* Methuen, 1984.

Jameson, Fredric. *Archaeologies of the Future: The Desire Called Utopia and Other Science Fictions.* Verso, 2005.

———. "Cognitive Mapping." In *Marxism and the Interpretation of Culture.* Eds. Cary Nelson and Lawrence Grossberg. U of Illinois P, 1988. 347–358

———. *Fables of Aggression: Wyndham Lewis, or, the Modernist as Fascist.* Berkeley: U of California P, 1979.

———. *The Geopolitical Aesthetic: Cinema and Space in the World System*. The British Film Institute and Indiana UP, 1992.

———. "Introduction." *The Ideologies of Theory, Volume 1: Situations of Theory*. U of Minnesota P, 1988. xxv–xxix.

———. *The Political Unconscious: Narrative as a Socially Symbolic Act*. Cornell UP, 1981.

———. *Postmodernism, or, the Cultural Logic of Late Capitalism*. Duke UP, 1991.

———. "The Vanishing Mediator; or, Max Weber as Storyteller." *Ideologies of Theory*. Verso, 2008. 309–343.

Kane, Douglass Charles. *Arda Reconstructed: The Creation of the Published Silmarillion*. Lehigh UP, 2011.

Kermode, Frank. *The Sense of an Ending: Studies in the Theory of Fiction*. Oxford UP, 1967.

Kisor, Yvette. "'Poor Sméagol': Gollum as Exile in Middle-earth." In *Tolkien in the New Century: Essays in Honor of Tom Shippey*. Eds. John Wm. Houghton, Janet Brennan Croft, Nancy Martsch, John D. Rateliff, and Robin Anne Reid. Jefferson, NC: McFarland & Company, 2014. 153–168.

Lafargue, Paul. "Reminiscences of Marx." In *Marx and Engels on Literature and Art: A Selection of Writings*. Eds. Lee Baxandall and Stefan Morawski. Telos Press, 1973. 150–151.

Lakowski, Romuald I. "The Fall and Repentance of Galadriel." In *Perilous and Fair: Women in the Works and Life of J. R. R. Tolkien*. Eds. Janet Brennan Croft and Leslie A. Donovan. Mythopoeic Press, 2015. 153–167.

Lukács, Georg. *The Historical Novel*. Trans. Hannah and Stanley Mitchell. U of Nebraska P, 1983.

———. *The Theory of the Novel*. Trans. Anna Bostock. MIT P, 1971.

Luling, Virginia. "An Anthropologist in Middle-earth." *Mallorn: The Journal of the Tolkien Society* 33 (1995): 53–57.

Lynch, Kevin. *The Image of the City*. MIT P, 1960.

Marx, Karl. *The Eighteenth Brumaire of Louis Bonaparte*. Trans. anon. International Publishers, 1963.

———. *Grundrisse: Foundations of the Political Economy*. Trans. Martin Nicolaus. Penguin, 1973.

Marx, Karl, and Friedrich Engels. *The Communist Manifesto*. Trans. Samuel Moore. Signet, 1998.

Mendlesohn, Farah, and Edward James. *A Short History of Fantasy*. Middlesex University Press, 2009.

Miéville, China. "Cognition as Ideology: A Dialectic of SF." *Red Planets: Marxism and Science Fiction.* Eds. Marc Bould and China Miéville. Wesleyan UP, 2009. 231–248.

———. "Introduction." *Historical Materialism* 10.4 (2002): 39–49.

Mitchell, Sebastian. *Utopia and Its Discontents: Plato to Atwood.* Bloomsbury 2020.

Moorcock, Michael. *Wizardry and Wild Romance: A Study of Epic Fantasy.* Victor Gollancz Ltd., 1987.

Moretti, Franco. *The Modern Epic: The World System from Goethe to Garcia-Márquez.* Verso, 1994.

Pearce, Joseph. *Tolkien, Man and Myth: A Literary Life.* HarperCollins, 1998.

Pratchett, Terry. *The Color of Magic.* Harper, 1989.

———. "Why Gandalf Never Married" (1985): http://www.ansible.co.uk/misc/tpspeech.html.

Rabkin, Eric S. *The Fantastic in Literature.* Princeton University Press, 1976.

Rateliff, John D. *The History of the Hobbit.* 2 vols. Houghton Mifflin, 2007.

———. "Inside Literature: Tolkien's Exploration of Medieval Genres." In *Tolkien in the New Century: Essays in Honor of Tom Shippey.* Eds. John Wm. Houghton, Janet Brennan Croft, Nancy Martsch, John D. Rateliff, and Robin Anne Reid. McFarland & Company, 2014. 133–152.

Reid, Robin Anne. "Race in Tolkien Studies: A Bibliographic Essay." In *Tolkien and Alterity.* Eds. Christopher Vaccaro and Yvette Kisor. Palgrave Macmillan, 2017. 33–74.

Rosebury, Brian. *Tolkien: A Cultural Phenomenon.* Palgrave, 2003.

Serge, Victor. *Memoires of the Revolutionary.* Trans. Peter Sedgwick and George Paizis. New York Review of Books, 2012.

Shippey, Tom. *J.R.R. Tolkien: Author of the Century.* Houghton Mifflin, 2000.

———. "Orcs, Wraiths, Wights: Tolkien's Images of Evil." *J.R.R. Tolkien and his Literary Resonances.* Ed. George Clark and Daniel Timmons. Greenwood, 2000. 183–98.

———. *The Road to Middle-earth: How J. R. R. Tolkien Created a New Mythology.* Houghton Mifflin, 2003.

Stanton, Michael N. *Hobbits, Elves, and Wizards: Exploring the Wonders and Worlds of J. R. R. Tolkien's* The Lord of the Rings. Palgrave, 2001.

Stuart, Robert. *Tolkien, Race, and Racism in Middle-earth.* Palgrave Macmillan, 2022.

Suvin, Darko. *Metamorphoses of Science Fiction: On the Poetics and History of a Literary Genre.* Yale UP, 1979.

Tally, Robert T., Jr. "Let Us Now Praise Famous Orcs." *Mythlore* 29.1/2 (2010): 17–28.

———. *Topophrenia: Place, Narrative, and the Spatial Imagination.* Indiana UP, 2019.

Terkel, Studs. *The Good War: An Oral History of World War II*. New Press, 1984.

Thomas, Paul Edmund. "Some of Tolkien's Narrators." In *Tolkien's "Legendarium": Essays on "The History of Middle-earth".* Edited by Verlyn Flieger and Carl F. Hostetter. Westport: Greenwood Press, 2000. 161–181.

Wilson, Edmund. "Oo, Those Awful Orcs!" *The Bit Between My Teeth: Literary Chronicles, 1950–1965.* Farrar, Strauss, and Giroux, 1965. 326–332.

Yeskov, Kirill. *The Last Ringbearer.* Trans. Yisroel Markov. Tenseg Press, 2011.

Young, Helen. *Race and Popular Fantasy Literature: Habits of Whiteness.* Routledge, 2016.

Vaccaro, Christopher, and Yvette Kisor, eds. *Tolkien and Alterity.* Palgrave Macmillan, 2017

Wise, Dennis Wilson. "On Ways of Studying Tolkien: Notes Toward a Better (Epic) Fantasy Criticism." *Journal of Tolkien Research* 9.1 (2020): https://scholar.valpo.edu/journaloftolkienresearch/vol9/iss1/2.

Index

© The Editor(s) (if applicable) and The Author(s), under exclusive
license to Springer Nature Switzerland AG 2022
R. T. Tally Jr., *J. R. R. Tolkien's* The Hobbit,
Palgrave Science Fiction and Fantasy: A New Canon,
https://doi.org/10.1007/978-3-031-11266-9